新日本民法典
新日本民法典講義（第２改訂版）

The New Japanese Civil Code:

as material for the study of comparative jurisprudence,

by *Nobushige Hozumi*

1904

新日本民法典

（東京帝国大学名誉教授・穂積陳重著）

PRINTED BY THE TOKYO PRINTING CO. LTD., TOKYO, JAPAN.

Lectures on the New Japanese Civil Code:

as material for the study of compatative jurisprudence,

by *Nobushige Hozumi*

Second & Revised Edition

1912

新日本民法典講義（第 2 改訂版）

（東京帝国大学名誉教授・穂積陳重著）

[Includes index]

THE MARUZEN KABUSHIKI-KAISHA, TOKYO, OSAKA & KYOTO.

学術選書プラス
5
民　法

2011 復刊

SHINZANSHA

信 山 社

新日本民法典

The New Japanese Civil Code:
as material for the study of comparative jurisprudence,

by ***Nobushige Hozumi***

1904

新日本民法典

（東京帝国大学名誉教授・穂積陳重著）

PRINTED BY THE TOKYO PRINTING CO. LTD., TOKYO, JAPAN.

学術選書プラス
5
民　法

2011 復刊

SHINZANSHA

信 山 社

THE

NEW JAPANESE CIVIL CODE,

AS MATERIAL FOR THE STUDY OF COMPARATIVE JURISPRUDENCE.

A PAPER READ AT

THE INTERNATIONAL CONGRESS OF ARTS AND SCIENCE,

AT THE

UNIVERSAL EXPOSITION, SAINT LOUIS 1904.

BY

NOBUSHIGE HOZUMI,

PROFESSOR OF LAW IN THE IMPERIAL UNIVERSITY OF TOKIO,
BARRISTER-AT-LAW, OF THE MIDDLE TEMPLE.

With the Compliments of

N. Hozumi.

AS MATERIAL FOR THE STUDY OF

COMPARATIVE JURISPRUDENCE.

A PAPER READ AT

THE INTERNATIONAL CONGRESS OF ARTS AND SCIENCE,

AT THE

UNIVERSAL EXPOSITION, SAINT LOUIS 1904.

BY

NOBUSHIGE HOZUMI,

PROFESSOR OF LAW IN THE IMPERIAL UNIVERSITY OF TOKIO,
BARRISTER-AT-LAW, OF THE MIDDLE TEMPLE.

ERRATA.

Page	4.	19th	Line, for	*religions*	read	*religious.*
,,	7.	26th	,, , ,,	*lawyer*	,,	*lawyers.*
,,	20.	32nd	,, , ,,	*governours*	,,	*governors.*
,,	23.	7th	,, , ,,	*in rem*	,,	*in personam.*
,,	26.	15th	,, , ,,	*priminary*	,,	*primary.*
,,	27.	17th	,, , ,,	*concepson*	,,	*conception.*
,,	33.	1st	,, , ,,	*lemitative*	,,	*limitative.*
,,	47.	25th	,, , ,,	*consin*	,,	*cousin.*
,,	52.	32nd	,, , ,,	*np*	,,	*up.*
,,	56.	24th	,, , ,,	*continzency*	,,	*contingency.*
,,	58.	3rd	,, , ,,	*housemembers*	,,	*house-members.*
,,	66.	9th	,, , ,,	*famale*	,,	*female.*

THE
NEW JAPANESE CIVIL CODE,
AS MATERIAL FOR THE STUDY OF
COMPARATIVE JURISPRUDENCE.

A PAPER READ AT

THE INTERNATIONAL CONGRESS OF ARTS AND SCIENCE,

AT THE

UNIVERSAL EXPOSITION, SAINT LOUIS 1904.

BY

NOBUSHIGE HOZUMI,

PROFESSOR OF LAW IN THE IMPERIAL UNIVERSITY OF TOKIO,
BARRISTER-AT-LAW, OF THE MIDDLE TEMPLE.

PRINTED BY THE TOKYO PRINTING CO., LTD., TOKYO, JAPAN.

The New Japanese Civil Code, as Material for the Study of Comparative Jurisprudence.

In responding to the call of the Comittee of the Congress to deliver a lecture on Comparative Law, I have, for reasons which will not be far to seek, taken the new Japanese Civil Code as the subject of my discourse. If, at the outset, I may be allowed to use a paradoxical expression in characterizing that law-book, I should say that "the East and the West, the Past and the Present meet in the new Japanese Civil Code." I mean that the codification of private law in Japan was the result of the great political and social revolution, which followed the opening of the country and the introduction of Western ideas; so that the Code embodies in itself both archaic and modern elements on the one hand, and Oriental and Occidental elements on the other. It is, so to speak, a connecting link between the Past and the Present, between the East and the West, and stands at the cross-roads of historical and comparative jurisprudence. It is, on that account, peculiarly interesting to scientific jurists, as supplying them with materials which few other systems can furnish. It will be my endeavour, in this lecture, to show the effect which the contact of the Western civilization with that of the East has produced on the civil law of the country, thereby illustrating some of the leading principles of the evolution of law by reference to the rules of the Code. The scope of my lecture being so wide, and the time for its delivery being limited, I shall confine myself to those characteristic features of the Code, which are not usually found in Occidental jurisprudence.

I. Causes of the Codification.

In order to set forth the characteristics of the Japanese Civil Code, it will be useful, first of all, briefly to explain the causes which led to the codification, and give a short sketch of the history of its compilation. The causes which led to the reform and codification of the civil law are principally two.

The first is to be found in the great *social and political changes*, which have taken place since the opening of the country to foreign intercourse, especially since the Restoration of the Emperor to actual power in 1868. It was just half a century ago, that Commondore Perry knocked at our doors to open the country to foreign trade. Aroused from the deep slumber of centuries, we rubbed our eyes, and saw Western civilization confronting us, but it was some time before we were wide awake, and realized the advantage of introducing it into our country.

In a country which had remained entirely secluded for centuries from the rest of the world, it was quite natural, that distrust, which in many cases grew to be hatred, of foreigners should, at first, have existed among the mass of the people; and that the cry of "jō-i" or "the Expulsion of foreigners" should have been raised among them. Many far-sighted statesmen and scholars, however, clearly saw the necessity of introducing Western civilization and of adopting whatever seemed conducive to the intellectual or material progress of the country, in order that Japan might become a member of the family of nations. There were others, who, while understanding very well the necessity of introducing Western civilization, joined the anti-foreign party, in order to hasten the overthrow of the Shogunate Government, for the expressions "Sonnō-jōi" or "Loyalty to the Emperor, and the expulsion of forcigners," although they had no necessary connection with one another were, at that time, adopted as watchwords by the party of political reform, in order to set the mass of the people against the Shogun's government. But, as soon as their object was attained, and the present Emperor was restored to real power, they threw off the mask and kept only the former half of their watch-word "Sonnō" or "Loyalty to the Emperor."

The first act of the Emperor, on ascending the throne, was to enunciate the fundamental principles of his government in the form of a solemn oath, which has since then been known as "the Five Articles of the Imperial Oath." The Emperor declared in this oath,

(1) That deliberative assemblies should be established and all measures of government should be decided by public opinion.

(2) That all classes, high and low, should unite in vigorously carrying out the plan of the government.

(3) Officials, civil and military, and all common people should, as far as possible, be allowed to fulfill their just desires, so that there might not be any discontent among them.

(4) Uncivilized customs of former times should be broken through, and everything should be based upon the just and equitable principle of nature.

(5) That *knowledge should be sought for throughout the world*, so that the welfare of the Empire might be promoted.

This oath has been made the basis of our national policy. How well the Emperor kept his oath, and how unswervingly his government and his people have followed the wish expressed by their soveregin, is shown by the subsequent events of our history.

The Feudal System was abolished, and all the Daimios or feudal lords voluntarily surrendered their fiefs to the Emperor, together with their powers to make laws, issue paper-currency and exercise both civil and criminal jurisdiction within their dominions. The four hereditary classes of the people, namely the Samurai or soldiers, farmers, artisans and merchants were abolished, and all could freely choose their own profession or calling. Officials were no longer appointed on account of birth, as was formerly the case, but on account of personal merits, and even the lowest born could aspire to become the highest official of the State. The family system was, as I shall show presently, gradually weakened, so that the individual began to take the place of the family as the unit of society. Schools for both sexes, have been established in all parts of the Empire, which are open to all classes without the least distinction. Higher education is no longer the monopoly of the Samurai and the clergy. Students and officials, have been yearly sent to Europe and America, to study different branches of art and science, or to investigate and report upon the methods and resources of Western civilization. Christianity which had been very strictly forbidden during the Tokugawa Shogunate, was gradually tolerated under the new government of the Emperor, until, at last, freedom of religions belief and worship was secured by Art. 28 of the Constitution promulgated in 1889. The introduction of steamships, railroads, electric telegraphs etc. completely changed the means of communication and travelling both on land and sea. The opening of foreign trade and the changes in commerce and industry at home, by the establishment of banking and other commercial firms and factories in differents parts of the country, brought about great economical revolutions among the people. The Imperial Household abolished the old ceremonial costumes, and adopted European dress for ceremonial occasions both for men and women. The men cut off their top-knots and had their hair dressed in Western fashion; they discarded their loose native dress and began to wear tight practical European dress; they now build their government offices, schools and other public buildings in European style; they began to eat beef, the partaking of which had been regarded as something sacrilegious. It is needless to say that these political, economical and social revolutions, which extended to every department of life, occasioned the necessity for corresponding reforms in the laws of the country, which could not be met by fragmentary legislations. Sweeping legislation by way of codification was the only way of keeping up with the rapid strides, which Japan had taken during the past three decades.

The second and more immediate cause of the codification of the civil law was the earnest desire on the part of the Japanese people to put an end to the existence of the *extra-territorial jurisdiction* which had been granted by earlier treaties to the sixteen Treaty Powers of Europe and America, and to resume the civil and criminal jurisdiction over the subjects and citizens of the Treaty Powers, residing or travelling in the country. At the time, that we first entered into commercial treaties with Western Powers, it was quite natural and reasonable, that they should demand the reservation to themselves of jurisdiction over their own respective subjects and citizens. This was indeed necessitated by the great difference between their own laws and institutions and those of Japan, while the habits and customs of the people were also quite unlike. We saw the necessity and justice of acceding to their demand, but, at the same time, felt that the existence of such a legal anomaly was a disgrace to the country, and wholly imcompatible with that scrupulous regard for the integrity of territorial sovereignty, which ought to characterize the intercourse of independent friendly nations. So, from an early date in the present reign, attempts were repeatedly made to revise the treaties and expunge from them the abominable extra-territorial clause. But, every time, we were met by the objection that our laws were incomplete. Although as a matter of principle, we did not admit the justice of the foreigners' objection to obeying the laws of the country to which they chose to resort, we were obliged, in fairness, to recognize the reasonableness of their objections.

After many years of difficult diplomatic negotiations, it was at last agreed, that the treaties should be revised and the extra-territoriality should be abolished; and, at the same time, the Japanese government undertook to frame codes of laws and put them in operation before the new treaties should go into effect.

The above-mentioned two causes, one internal and the other external, combined to make the work of codification one of the most urgent necessities of the time. As a preliminary step to the work of codification, a Bureau for the Investigation of Institutions was established in the third Year of Meiji (1870) and one of the fruits of the labour of that Bureau was the translation of the French Codes. This translation afforded the knowledge-thirsty Japanese ideas of Western laws for the first time, and had an immense influence upon subsequent legislation and judicial dicisions in the courts of law. In 1875, a Committee for the Compilation of the Civil Code was appointed for the first time. In 1878, a draft was submitted by this Committee to the Government. This draft was a close imitation of the French Civil Code, both in its arrangements and in its content, and was not adopted by the Government. In 1880, Prof. Boissonade, an eminent French jurist, who was then a legal adviser to the Japanese Government, was asked to prepare a new draft, and in the next year, a Bureau for the Codification of the Civil Law was established, to which Prof. Boissonade's draft was submitted for deliberation. The Bureau was abolished in 1886, and a Committee for the Investigation of Law was appointed, composed of the members of the Genrōin or the Senate and of the Bench, with Count Yamada, the Minister of Justice, at its head. This committee made its report in 1888, and the draft was submitted to the deliberation of the Senate and was adopted by that Council. On the 27th of March, 1890, under Law No. 28, those parts of the Code which were drafted by Prof. Boissonade, that is, Book II, relating to "Property in General," Book III, relating to the "Means of Acquiring Property," Book IV, "Security of Rights *in personam*" and Book V, relating to "Evidence" were published. Those parts which were prepared by Japanese jurists, namely, Book I, relating to "Persons" and part of Book III, relating to "Succession" were published on the 16th of October of the same year; and the whole Code was to go into operation from the 1st of January 1893.

Thus after the arduous toil of fifteen years, Japan possessed a code of private law for the first time in her history. It was quite natural that the Code should become a topic of earnest consideration for all educated classes of the people. Especially among lawyers and politicians, a violent controversy arose regarding the merits of the new Code. Those jurists, who had studied English law in the Tokio University or in England or America, first raised their voices against the Code and demanded the postponement of the date of its going into operation, with a view to its complete revision. The French section of Japanese lawyers, on the other hand, supported the Code and insisted upon the necessity of its going into operation at the date originally appointed. The German section of jurists, whose number was at that time comparatively small, was divided into two parties, some siding with the one, others joining the other. Japanese lawyer were thus divided into two hostile camps, and the lively discussion which arose among them, is known as the "Postponement Campaign." The arguments pro and con put forward for the postponement and revision of the Code were many and were of varying inportance. To outsiders, the campaign may have seemed like a sectarian conflict between the English and French groups of Japanese lawyers. But this struggle is eminently interesting to scientific observers of the general history of law, for it was, in reality, a contest of the Historical School with the School of Natural Law, resembling in many respects the famous controversy between Savigny and Thibaut in the beginning of the same century. This question contained an important issue, as to which theory should have a predominant influence over the jurisprudence and legislation of the country.

In order to explain this interesting event in our legal history, I must, for a moment, stop to give an account of the state of legal education in Japan at that time. English law had been taught in the Imperial University of Tokio since 1874 by English, American and Japanese teachers, and also in other law schools, and a great number of the graduates had, by that time, already filled important positions on the Bench and at the Bar as well as in other places, both in and out of the Government. They were all taught the doctrines of Bentham, Austin and Maine, and most of them belonged to the school of positive law. On the other hand, there was a law school attached to the Department of Justice, in which French Law was taught by Prof. Boissonade and other French and native teachers. There were also two or three private law schools in which French law was taught. The graduates of these schools, who also filled important positions, had been taught the doctrines of Natural Law. It was quite natural that the doctrines which lawyers had imbibed in their early days of studentship should have strongly influenced their views as to legislations in their maturer days. And thus arose two opposite schools among the lawyers of Japan. In 1887, just three years before the publication of the Civil Code, the Imperial University made a reform in the program of the College of Law. The French Law School of the Department of Justice was transferred to the University, and at the same time, a German Law Section was newly established, so that there came to be three sections in the College of Law, besides a fourth which is devoted to

Political Science. This tripartite division in the University law education could not fail to produce an enduring effect on the subsequent legislation of the country. The Civil Code had become law, before the Constitution came into force in 1890, and the question of the postponement of its operation had to be decided in the Imperial Diet. Accordingly, a bill was introduced at the session of 1892 in the House of Representatives to postpone the operation of the Code with a view to its revision. After several warm debates, the bill was passed by both Houses of the Imperial Diet and the operation of the Code was postponed by Law No 8. until the 31st of December 1896. Thus, the so-called "Postponement Campaign" resulted in the victory of the "Postponement Party;" and in the following year, a Codification Committee was established by an Imperial Edict. The constitution of this Committee affords a very important clue for understanding the character of the new Code. The committee, with Marquis Ito, then the prime minister, as its president, consisted of members of both Houses of the Diet, professors of the Imperial University, members of the Bench and the Bar, with other eminent jurists and leading representatives of commerce and industry. The number of the members varied from time to time, but throughout, care had been taken in the appointment of members to represent every interest in society and also to represent English, French and German Schools of Japanese lawyers. The "Postponement Campaign" was very fierce while it lasted, but when the question was once settled, both parties threw off their animosity and joined hands in the work of giving the nation a code which would meet the exigencies of the time. The appointment of the three special members to prepare the draft also shows a conciliatory spirit on all sides. Professors Tomii, Ume and myself were appointed to prepare the original draft which was to be submitted to the deliberation of the Committee. Professor Tomii, although he had studied law in Paris and is *docteur en droit*, and thus belonged to the French School, sided with the " Postponement Party," and not only formed a remarkable exception among his comrades, but was one of the staunch advocate of postponement and revision. Professor Ume, who had studied law in Lyon and is also *docteur en droit*, was one of the champions of the "Anti-Postponement Party." I myself studied English law in the Inns of Court in London and am a member of the English Bar; and I belonged to the Postponement Party. Both Prof. Ume and I also studied law in the University of Berlin, after we had finished our courses in France and England respectively. Thus, it will be seen that two out of the three framers of the Code represented the French Section, but one of them belonged to the Postponement Party. While two belonged to the French and one to the English School, two of them had studied German law.

The constitution of the Committee, especially that of the Drafting Committee made it clear, that they could not agree to take the law of any one country as an exclusive model upon which to frame the new Code. Prof. Boissonade's Code was principally based upon the French Civil Code, but the framers of the revised Code agreed to collect the codes, statutes, and judicial reports of all civilized countries which existed in the English, French, German or Italian Languages, besides international treaties which have reference to the rules of private law. They accordingly collected more than thirty civil codes, including many drafts, such as the draft of the Civil Code of New York, the draft of the Greman Code, the drafts of the Belgian Code, besides other codes, statutes, reports and treaties; and comparing the rules or principles which exist in different countries, adopted whatever seemed to be best suited to the requirements of the country. In the original draft which was submitted to the deliberation of the Committee, an explanation was attached to each article, stating the reasons for the adoption of the rule. The corresponding articles or rules which exist in other countries as well as rules, precedents and customs in our own country were also cited for the consideration of the Committee. This method of preparing the draft gave a characteristic feature to the new Code. The Japanese Civil Code may be said to be a *fruit of comparative jurisprudence*. At first sight, it may appear that the new Code was very closely modeled upon the new German Civil Code; and I have very often read statements to that effect. It is true that the first and second draft of the German Code furnished very valuable material to the drafting committee and had a great influence upon the deliberations of the Committee. But, on close examination of the principles and rules adopted in the Code, it will appear that they gathered materials from all parts of the civilized world and freely adopted rules or principles from the laws of any country, whenever they saw the advantage of doing so. In some parts, rules were adopted from the French Civil Code; in others, the principles of English common law were followed; in others again, such laws as the Swiss Federal Code of Obligations of 1881, the new Spanish Civil Code of 1889, the Property Code of Montenegro, Indian Succession and Contract Acts or the Civil Codes of Louisiana, Lower Canada or the South American Republics or the draft Civil Code of New York, and the like have given materials for the framers of the Code. In January 1896, the report of the Committee on Book I, "General Provisions," Book II, "Rights *in rem*" and Book III, "Rights *in personam*" was submitted to the Imperial Diet and was adopted with only a few unimportant modifications. In April of the same year, these three Books were promulgated as Law No. 89. The remaining two Books on "Family" and "Succession" were submitted to the Imperial Diet in May 1898 and adopted by both Houses with only slight modifications, and were promulgated as Law No. 9 in June; and the whole Codes came into force on the 16th of July 1898.

The foregoing sketch, brief as it is, of the history of the

codification of the civil law wlll be sufficient to show that the new Japanese Civil Code is the result of the comparative study of laws, and offers in its turn, valuable materials for the study of comparative jurisprudence.

II. Objects of the Codification.

I think it may be laid down as a general rule regarding the evolution of law, that *a comprehensive legislation generally follows a great social revolution.* If laws are social phenomena, it is quite natural that social changes should always bring with them corresponding changes in the laws of the country. The legal history of all nations, either ancient or modern, shows that the objects sought to be obtained by codification fall under one of the following four heads ; namely, Pacification, Innovation, Unification and Simplification.

(1) Sometimes, codification takes place after a great social disturbance in order *to restore peace and maintain order by means of comprehensive legislation.* This was true of the ancient codes of Draco and Solon in Greece, the Law of Twelve Tables in Rome, and the codifications in China since the Han Dynasty, where it was customary for the founder of every dynasty to publish a new code of laws after he had gained the imperial power by force of arms. In Japan, the Codes of the Hōjō and the Tokugawa belong to this class.

(2) Laws are often codified either *to bring about a social reform*, or *to adjust the law to the requirements of the new state of things*, which has been brought about by social reform. To this class belong most of the codes, which have been promulgated in Japan since the Restoration of 1868.

(3) Very often codification takes place with a view to *the*

unification of different local laws and customs, so that the country may be governed by a uniform code of laws. One of the objects of the Code Napoleon, the Italian Civil Code of 1865, and the new German Imperial Codes was, in each case, the unification of the laws of the country. It was the principal object of the first Japanese Criminal Code of 1870, which was published soon after the Restoration to establish unity in criminal law throughout the Empire, by abolishing the particular laws which existed within the jurisdictions of the Daimios.

(4) Simplification of law by means of *logical arrangement* or *consolidation* of legal rules constitutes the most usual motive for codification in modern states.

Now, the majority of codifications, except sometimes those coming under the fourth class just mentioned, take place after great political or social revolutions, in consequence of which, pacification, innovation, unification or simplification becomes necessary. The history of codification in Japan amply exemplifies the above statement. The promulgation of the Taihō Codes of 702 A. D. was the result of the great political and social revolution, which followed the introduction of Chinese civilization into the country. The next great codification, the framing of the Jōyei Shikimoku in 1232 A. D. under the Hojō Regency, was necessitated by the great political and social changes, which had taken place since the establishment of the Feudal System under the military government of the Shōguns. The new Japanese Civil Code is, as I have explained above, the result of the revolution which followed the opening of the country to foreign intercoure. Thus, *each of the three great epochs in Japanese history, the introduction of Chinese civilization, the establishment of Feudalism and the introduction of Western civilization, has been followed by codification.* The chief object of the Taihō Code, belonging to the first period, was Innovation; that of the Jōyei

Shikimoku, belonging to the second period, was Pacification; while the framing of the new Civil Code had for its objects Innovation and Unification as well as Simplification.

III. Methods of Comparative Jurisprudence.

Looked at from another point of view, the new Japanese Civil Code may be taken as an illustration of the effect which the contact of Western with Eastern civilization has produced on the laws and institutions of the country. In this respect, I must first say a few words as to the methods of Comparative Jurisprudence. Hitherto, there have been three methods of comparison in vogue. One of them takes the *law of a particular state* as the unit of comparison, and comparing with it the laws of different states, finds similarities and divergencies among them, and deduces from them certain principles of law. This is the method generally adopted by jurists. In France, for instance, where comparative law is studied with greatest zeal, valuable materials for this method of investigation are furnished by the publications of the laws of different countries in the "Bulletin" and "Annuaire" of the "Société de législation comparée" and by the numerous translations of foreign codes by Foucher, Antoine St. Joseph, Lehr, Dareste, Grasserie, Levé, Turrel, Prudhomme, Lepelletier and other eminent jurists.

There are others, who, perceiving that there are common features in the laws of each *race*, take a wider basis for their investigation and make the laws of particular races the units of comparison, and compare the one with the other.

There are others again, who take a still wider basis, and compare legal phenomena of different peoples without regard to nationality or race.

Of these three methods, the first may compare, for instance,

English law with French, the second Germanic laws with Slavonic laws, while the third takes up, perhaps, the marriage laws and customs of European nations, American Indians, African negroes, Australians and Chinese.

All these three methods of comparison, which I have mentioned above, are useful and legitimate methods of investigating the principles of law; and none of them can be rejected to the exclusive adoption of the other. But I think another method can be added to the list, which, though not hitherto employed, may be very advantageously adopted in the investigations of general principles of law. I mean a method which takes for the unit of comparison a certain group of laws having a *common lineage* or *descent*. If we examine the laws of different countries which have made a certain progress in civilization, we shall find that the law of each country consists of *two elements*; namely, the *indigenous element* and the *foreign element*; and except in uncivilized or barbarous communities which have no intellectual intercourse with other countries, instances are very rare, in which the law of any country is found consisting exclusively of indigenous elements. With the progress of means of communication and the consequent increase of intercourse among different peoples, the exchange, not only of material, but also of intellectual products becomes greater; and in regard to law, it may be laid down as a general rule that the higher the community stands in the scale of civilization, the greater is the proportion of the foreign to the indigenous element. This comes from what is called the reception or adoption of foreign laws.

Now, when the rules or principles of law of one country are adopted in another, there arises a sort of *kinship* between the laws of those two countries. One is descended from the other, and the *relationship, as it were, of ancestor and descendant is created between them.* The old law which served as a model or source of the new law may be called the "Parental Law" or "Mother-law" in relation to the new, which stands in a filial relation to the parental law.

The law of one country may be adopted in other countries *directly*, as Roman law was received in Germany, or *indirectly*, that is, it may be first adopted in one country, and then through that country, it may be received in the third, as European law, which has first been received in Japan, is now being introduced through her in China and Corea. Or again, the law of a mother country may be extended to her colonies or dependencies, as in the case with English law in British colonies.

In this way, the laws of all civilized countries may be divided into several groups, each comprising laws of many countries, but having common features and characteristics owing to their common origin. These different groups may be compared one with another, in order to find out uniformities and divergencies among them, and thus establish general principles of law. This method of comparative study of law, which may be called the *Genealogical Method*, to distinguish it from the other three, has the advantage, among many others, of combining the historical with the comparative method.

IV. Great Families of Law.

If, in order to take the Genealogical Method of comparison, we classify the laws existing at present in different parts of the world, we shall find that there are at least seven Great Families of Laws; namely, (1) the Family of Chinese Law, (2) the Family of Hindu Law, (3) the Family of Mohamedan Law, (4) the Family of Roman Law, (5) the Family of Germanic Law, (6) the Family of Slavonic Law, and (7) the Family of English Law. I have called these groups "the *Great Families of Laws*," because this classification is not meant to be exhaustive or exclusive. There are many smaller branches of law, not belonging to any of the above mentioned Families, which are, none the less, very important for the Genealogical Method of comparative study, but for the purpose of the present lecture, they need not be mentioned here.

V. The Position of the Japanese Civil Code among Legal Systems of the World.

I have been at some length in explaining this method of comparative jurisprudence, in order to show the position of the new Japanese Civil Code in the general legal history of the world. Since the first introduction of Chinese civilization into our country, and the consequent Reform of the Taika Era (646 A.D.), the work of which was completed by the publication of the famous Taihō-Codes in 701 A. D., *Japanese law has belonged to the Family of Chinese Law* for more than one thousand six hundred years; and notwithstanding many great changes in the laws and institutions of the country, which have taken place, since that time, the basis of Japanese laws and institutions has always been Chinese moral philosophy, together with the custom of Ancestor-worship and the Feudal system.

The Criminal Code (Shin-ritsu-koryō) which was published in 1870, three years after the Restoration of 1868, was modeled upon the Chinese Codes of Tang, Min, and Shin Dynasty with certain modifications suggested by old Japanese laws. Only three years later, that code was revised, and a new code was published under the title of the Revised Criminal Code (Kaitei-Ritsurei). In the framing of that new Code, some European codes, especially the French, were consulted and adopted to a certain extent. Now, these two codes mark the transition period in the history of Japanese law. *The former was the last in the Chinese, and the latter the first in the European, system of legislation.* The Japanese law was at that time rapidly passing *from the Family of Chinese law to the Family of European laws.*

From the beginning of the present reign, the Imperial government was very active in making laws to meet the exigencies of the new state of things. But finding that such fragmentary legislation could not keep pace with the rapid progress of the nation and meet the requirements of the changing circumstances, the Daijōkwan, or the Great Council of State, which was then the supreme legislature, issued a Law (No. 103 in the Eighth year of Meiji, 1875) which provided in art. 3, that judges should decide civil cases according to the express provisions of written law, and in cases where there was no such written law, according to custom. In the absence of both written and customary laws, they were to decide *according to the principles of reason and justice.* This law flung wide open the door for the ingress of foreign law, and marks an epoch in Japanese legal history. Now, by this time, translations of the French Codes and other law books had appeared, and there were some judges on the Bench, though comparatively few at that time, who had studied English or French law. The rapidly changing circumstances of Japanese society brought many cases before the court, for which there were no express rules, written or customary, and the judges naturally sought to find out "the principles of reason and justice" in Western jurisprudence. The older members of the Bench, who had not been systematically taught in Western jurisprudence, consulted the translations of the French and other European Codes and text books, while the younger judges who had received systematic legal education in the Universities, either at home or abroad, and whose number increased from year to year, consulted Western Codes, statute books, law reports, and juridical treatises, and freely applied the principles of

Occidental jurisprudence, which in their opinion, were conformable to reason and justice. Blackstone, Kent, Pollock, Anson, Langdel, Windscheid, Dernburg, Mourlon, Baudry-Lacantinerie and other text books and the numerous commentaries on European Codes, statute books and law reports were looked upon as repositories of just and reasonable principles and supplied necessary data for their judgements. In this manner, Occidental jurisprudence entered our country, not only indirectly through the *University* and other law colleges, but also directly through the *Bench* and the *Bar*.

The above law, bold as it was, was only meant to be a temporary measure to supply the immediate wants of the changing society, until a complete and systematic code should have been compiled. In the meantime, the work of codification had been steadily proceeding, and resulted in the promulgation of the Criminal Code and the Code of Criminal Procedure in 1880, the Revised Code of Criminal Procedure, and the Code of Civil Procedure in 1890, the new Civil Code in 1896 and 1898, and Commercial Code in 1899.

What I have said above, will suffice to show that the new Japanese Civil Code stands in a filial relation to the European systems, and *with the introduction of Western civilization, the Japanese civil law passed from the Chinese Family to the Roman Family of law.*

VI. The Publication of the Code.

One of the most remarkable changes which the introduction of Western jurisprudence produced in Japan was the change in the *conception of law*. Previous to the Restoration of 1868, *there was no idea that publication was essential to law*. On the contrary, during the time of the Tokugawa Shogunate, most laws, especially the criminal code, were *kept in strict secrecy.* They were all in manuscript and were neither allowed to be printed nor published; and none but the judges and officials who were charged with the duty of carrying the rules into effect were allowed the perusal of the codes and the records of judicial precedents.

The famous Criminal Code of the Tokugawa Shogunate, commonly known as the "Hyakka-jō" or "The Hundred Articles" bears the following injunction at the end:—

"The above rules have been settled with His Highness' gracious sanction, and nobody except the magistrates shall be allowed to peruse them." The subsequent compilation, called "Kwajō-rui-ten" contains the same injunction with the following addition:—

"Moreover, it is forever forbidden to make extracts from this Code, even of one article thereof." In 1841, thirteen authentic manuscript copies of the Code were made, and all the other copies and extracts which the clerks had made for their own use were ordered to be produced and burnt. One Ono Gonnojō and his son were severely punished for publishing a book which contained the "Hundred Articles" of the Code. An owner of a certain circulating library who had a manuscript book, showing the days on which the magistrates transacted business, or the "*dies fasti*" and "*nefasti*" of the judicial court, was punished with banishment from his place of abode. These and many other like cases which occured during the Tokugawa Shogunate show in what strict secrecy some parts of the laws were kept in those times.

The Taihō Code of 702, Jōyei-Shikimoku of 1232 and other old laws before the time of the Tokugawa Shogunate were printed and distributed *among officials* of the Imperial or the Shogunate Government, the governours of provinces, chiefs of clans etc., but they were not published in the sense in which laws are published in the present day. The Jōyei-Shikimoku, which was the fundamental Code during the time of the Hōjō-Regency, concludes with an oath by the councilors, to the effect, that they would render justice with impartiality, and according to reason, and in case of disobedience to the rules and principles set forth in the Code, they would incur the wrath and the punishment of the gods. These laws were all *commands adressed to the officials, not to the people. They were rules for the conduct of officials, not rules of conduct for the citizen.* It was upon officials only, that law imposed the obligation to observe the rules of law in their relation to the people, whether they acted in administrative or in judicial capacity. The people were merely passive objects of the law, and it was their part implicitly to obey the commands of officials. Austin and others, who define law as a command of the lawgiver, mean thereby a command addressed to, and imposing obligations upon, the citizen. But in Japan, *this conception was only reached after the introduction of Occidental jurisprudence* into the country. Two legislative acts in the beginning of the present reign very clearly show this transition in the nature of law. The publication of the new Criminal Code "Shinritsu Koryō" in the 3rd year of Meiji marks the first step in the revolution of the legal idea. The policy of the Tokugawa Government was based upon the famous Chinese maxim "Let people abide by, but not be apprised of, the law." (民可使由之,不可使知之) and went so far as to keep the law in strict secrecy. Although the first Criminal Code was modeled upon Chinese Codes, the new Imperial Government took another and wiser Chinese maxim "To kill without previous instruction is cruetly" (不敎而殺虐也), and caused the new Code to be printed and published. I have said that the first Criminal Code was based upon the Chinese system and in the amended Code, the French Criminal Code was consulted. The comparison of the Imperial Proclamations which form the preambles to these two Codes is very interesting, as showing a great change in the conception of law, that took place during the three years which intervened between the first and the second Code. In the Imperial Proclamation which is prefixed to the first Code, His Majesty enjoins his *officials to observe the rules of the Code;* while in the Imperial Proclamation attached to the second Code, it is his *subjects as well as his officials* that are so commanded. In the same year with the publication of the second Code, that is 1873, a law was enacted (Ordinance 68. of 6th year of Meiji) in which it was declared that "henceforth every law shall, on its promulgation, be posted up in convenient places during thirty days *for the information of the people.*" Since that time, several laws have been passed, in which the same principle is carried farther, and now the publication which is made in the Official Gazette has become an essential step in giving them binding force.

We have now reached the *third stage* in the evolution of the idea of law. At present, according to Art. 37 of the Constitution, every law requires the consent of both Houses of the Imperial Diet. Of the five Codes, which have been promulgated, the new Civil Code was the first which became law under the new constitutional government, and therefore, with the consent of the Diet.

From what I have said above, it will be seen that there are *three stages* observable in the development of the idea of law. At first, publication was not essential to the binding force of the law. Laws were commands addressed to the *magistrates*, not to the people. The people were merely the *passive object of the operation of laws.* Next comes an epoch, when the laws become commands addressed to the *people*, and publication forms an essential element of the law. People become the *direct object* of the law, and a party, as it were, to its operation. In the third and final stage, the people not only become a *party to the operation of the law*, but a *party to the making of it* through their representatives.

VII. The Arrangement of the Code.

The Civil Code drafted by Prof. Boissonade, which became law but never went into operation, was divided into the following five books; namely, Book I, "Persons"; Book II, "Property in General"; Book III, "Means of Acquiring Property"; Book IV, "Security of Rights *in rem*"; and Book V, "Evidence." The objections which were raised against this arrangement were many, some from scientific, others from practical, points of view; but it is needless to mention them here. Some will appear when I come to compare it with the arrangement of the new Code. The framers of the latter did not follow the arrangement of the first Code, nor did they adopt the classifications of the French or other codes based upon the Institutes of Justinian.

The new Civil Code is divided into the following five Books, according to the plan which German jurists call "Pandekten-System"; namely, Book I, "General Provisions"; Book II, "Rights *in rem*"; Book III, "Rights *in personam*"; Book IV, "Family" and Book V, "Succession." One of the reasons for rejecting the so-called "Institutionen-System," and adopting the "Pandekten-System" was that the latter system of arrangement was peculiarly suited to the present state of law in Japan.

The first Code, following the French Code, had no distinct portion assigned to general rules applicable to all other parts. This system rendered frequent repetition of the same rules necessary in different parts of the Code, thereby making the whole work a voluminous code, containing 1762 articles; while the new Code, following the Saxon Civil Code and the then draft of the German Civil Code, placed at the beginning all the general rules, relating to persons as subjects of rights, to things as objects of rights, and to facts and events by which rights are acquired, lost or transferred This method of arrangement avoided unnecessary repetitions and made the body of the law succinct; the new Code containing only 1146 articles.

The new Code, besides having a Book devoted to general provisions common to all legal relations, has distinct places set apart for the laws of Family and Succession. In the Code drafted by Prof. Boissonard the law of family was included in Book I relating to "Persons," and the law of succession formed a part of Book III relating to the "Means af Acquiring Property." Now, this arrangement formed one of the strong reasons for postponing the operation of the first Code and reconstructing it on an entirely new basis.

Before the Restoration it was the *family*, and *not the individual*, that formed the unit of society. The family was then a corporation; and as a general rule, only the house-head could hold public office or private property, or transact business, all other members of the family being dependent upon him. But since the Restoration, this state of things has changed, and the disintegration of the family is rapidly going on. The family has now ceased to be a corporation in the eyes of law, and the dependent members of the family or the house-members can hold office or property or transact business equally with its head Japanese society is now passing *from the stage of family-unit to the stage of individual-unit*. But still, the family occupies an important place in the social life of the people, and there are many rules which are peculiar to their family relations, and which ought, on that account, to be grouped together and separated from the rules relating to persons regarded simply as individuals. The "Pandekten-System" is peculiarly suited to this transient state of society, for it provides for the rules relating to persons in their capacity as individuals or members of a society in the General Part, and sets apart a distinct place for those rules which relate to person in their capacity as members of a family. In civilized societies, the rules which regard men as individuals belong to general law, while those which regard men in their family relations belong to particular law. But in less civilized communities, the case is just the reverse; the *family law may be said to form the general law*, the law relating to persons in their individual capacity falling under the category of *particular law*. Japan is now in a transition stage; so that the placing of the rules relating to individuals in the general part, and the rules relating to family relations in the particular part of the Code is, not only logically correct, but is especially suited to the present state of the Japan law.

As to the place of the Succession Law in the Code, strong objection was raised against the arrangement of Prof Boissonade which put it in Book III, under the head of " Means of Acquiring Property. In Japan, as I shall show presently, succession cannot, at least as regards the most usual kind of it, be regarded as a mode of acquiring property.

Comparative study of succession laws of different peoples in different degrees of civilization, shows that there are *three stages in the evolution* of this branch of law. In the first and earliest stage, succession is regarded as the mode of perpetuating the *worship* of ancestors; next comes the time when it is regarded as a mode of succeeding to the *status* of deceased persons; and it is only in the last stage, that succession becomes a mode of acquiring *property*.

Now in Japan, until recently, as the family was a corporation the only person who could hold property was the head of a house. Consequently the only kind of succession which was then recognized by law was " Katoku Sōzoku " or the *succession to the headship of a house*, which was the succession to status, and the house-property descended to the heir as an appendage to the status of the house-headship. It is only after house-members were allowed to have independent property, that succession which can properly be said to be succession to property began to be recognized. So, there are, at present, two kinds of succession, *status-succession* and *property-succession* existing side by side. The status-succession cannot be put under the category of the law of property, nor can the property-succession be put under the law of persons. The arrangement of the "Pandekten-System," which devotes a particurar Book to succession law at the end of the Code is peculiarly suited to this state of law, and recommended itself to the framers of the new Code in preference to the classification adopted by Prof. Boissonade.

VIII. The Introduction of the Notion of Right.

It will be seen, from what I have stated above, that the classification of rules in the new Civil Code is made upon the basis of *priminary distinctions regarding rights*. But the notion of right did not originally exist in Japan, before the introduction of Western jurisprudence. Many writers assume that right is coeval with law, and law and right are only two terms expressing the same notion from different points of view. Some even go so far as to affirm, that right is anterior to law, and the latter only exists for the assurance or protection of the former. In Japan, however, the idea of right did not exist so long as her laws belonged to the Chinese Family. There was indeed the notion of *duty* or *obligation*, but neither the notion of right nor the word for it existed either in Japanese or Chinese. The nearest approach to it in Japanese was perhaps "*bun*" which means "*share*" or "*portion.*" This word was frequently used to express the share or part which a person had in society and which he expected that society would recognize as his due. But this word was not quite definite in its meaning, and was more often used in a contrary sense, expressing a person's *duty*, or sometimes the *part* or *limit* which he ought not to exceed. So, when the notion of right was first introduced into Japan, there was no fit word to translate it, and a new word had to be coined to express this novel idea. The late Dr. Tsuda who had been sent to Holland by the Shogunate Government to study law in the University of Leyden, on his return to Japan published a book entitled "A Treatise on Western Public Law" in 1868, the year of the Restoration. In this book he used the new word "*ken-ri*" for right, which he coined by combining the words "*ken*" or "*power*" and "*ri*" or "*interest*." This word has since been received to express the notion of right. Sir John Lubbock in his book "On the Origine of Civilization" (ch. VIII) says that lower races are "deficient in the idea of right, though familiar with that of law," Sir Henry Maine says that "jus" among Roman lawyers generally meant not "a right" but "law;" and that Romans "constructed their memorable system without the help of the conceptson of legal right." I think it may be laid down as a general rule of the evolution of law, that *laws from being the rules of duty become the rules of right. Early laws impose duty but do not confer right.* But in the course of time, men begin to realize, that the benefit which results to any one on account of duty imposed upon another, is of greater importance than the duty itself; so that right which was at first only the *secondary notion* and nothing more than the reflection of duty, began to be regarded as the *primary* object of law. This change in the conception of law took place in Japan within the last forty years, and resulted in the classification of the rules of the Civil Code on the basis of right.

IX The Legal Position of Woman.

With reference to Book I of the Code, which relates to "General Provisions," I will only touch upon the subjects of the

Legal Position of Woman and that of *Foreigners*; for these are the two points where the Code has made greatest changes in that part of the law. I will first speak of woman.

Three periods may be distinguished in the history of Japan, as to the legal position of woman; the *first*, corresponding to the period during which our national law consisted solely of indigenous elements; the *second*, when Japanese law belonged to the Chinese Family of Law; and the *third* dating from the time when our law passed from the Chinese to the European Family of Law.

The first period extends from the beginning of our history to the introduction of Chinese civilization. During this period, women seem to have occupied a higher place than in later times, filling positions of importance and honor in state, religion and household. Perhaps, the higher position, which women occupied during the early period of our history, was due partly to the primitive simplicity and the absence of artificial doctrines, which later on assigned a subordinate position to women. The first Imperial Ancestor and the central figure in national worship is a goddess "Amaterasu Ō-mi-Kami" or the "Great Goddess of the Celestial Light." There was no law to prevent female members of the Imperial Family from ascending the throne, and there have been many Empresses who ruled the Empire. The Empress Jingō invaded and conquered Corea at the head of a large army.

With the conquest and subjugation of Corea by this "Empress of God-like Exploit" begins the second period in the history of the legal position of woman in Japan; for from this time, Chinese civilization began to enter Japan, first through Corea, and afterward from China directly. It was chiefly the doctrines of Chinese moral philosophy that changed the primitive state of comparative freedom and independence of woman, and placed her in an abnormally inferior position. The Chinese *doctrine of the perpetual obedience of woman* to the other sex is expressed in the precept of "the *three obediences*," (三從)—"obedience, while yet unmarried, to a father; obedience, when married, to a husband; obedience, when widowed, to a son."

It is curious to note, by the way, that an exact counterpart of this doctrine of three obediences is to be found in Hindoo Law. In one place Manu says "Day and night women must be kept in dependence by the males of their family" (Manu IX. 2. Buehler's transl.); and in another place "In childhood, a female must be subject to her father; in youth, to her husband; when her Lord is dead, to her sons." (V. 148)

Buddhism and Feudalism contributed to the keeping of woman in a state of dependence. Buddhism regards woman as an unclean creature, a temptation or snare to virtue and an obstacle to peace and holiness. Feudalism, which disdained anything effeminate, also regarded woman in the light of a temptation to courage and faithful performance of duty, and, although she was treated with kindness and consideration far above that received in other Asiatic countries, she did not command that romantic homage which the gallant knights of Mediæval Europe paid to the other sex. Prof. Chamberlain, one of the best authorities on Japan, writes:—"Japanese feudalism—despite its general similarity to the feudalism of the West—knew nothing of gallantry. A Japanese knight performed his valiant deeds for no such fanciful reward as a lady's smile. He performed them out of loyalty to his lord, or filial piety towards the memory of his papa."

Thus, these three factors, Chinese philosophy, Buddhism and Feudalism, combined to place the Japanese woman in a state of dependence during the second period. She could not become the head of a house; she could not hold property nor contract in her own name; she could not become a guardian of her own child; she could not adopt a child in her own name; in short, she had no independent status and was excluded from the enjoyment or exercise of almost all rights.

But in the third period, during which European civilization has been introduced, female education has spread throughout the country, Western jurisprudence has superseded Chinese, and Japanese law has become a member of the European Family of Laws, a great revolution has come over the social and legal position of woman. This reform was consummated by the publication of the new Civil Code. This Code "created the new legal woman" as an able writer on Japan has expressed it. (Clement's Modern Japan. ch. XIII.) It proceeds upon the principle of equality of the sexes, and makes no distinction between man and woman in their enjoyment and exercise of private rights, so long as the woman remains single. She may now become the head of a house, in which case all house-members, whether male or female,—even her husband when she is married—come under her power and are legally dependent upon her. She may exercise parental authority over her own child, if her husband be dead. She may adopt children either alone, when she is single or a widow, or in conjunction with her husband, when married. She may make any contract or acquire or dispose of property in her own name. In short, she may be a party to any legal transactions, as long as she remains *feme sole*. When she is married, her state of coverture obliges her to obtain the permission of her husband in doing certain acts, which may involve grave consequences upon their conjugal life; such as contracting debt, acquisition or loss of immovables or valuable moveables, instituting legal proceedings, accepting or renouncing succession, entering into contract of personal service etc. Even in regard to these acts, she can not be considered as laboring under legal incapacity, for when she does these acts without her husband's permission, they are not void, but only voidable, that is, liable to be annulled by her husband (Civil Code Art. 14.). With her husband's permission, she may also engage in business, in which case, she is considered in regard thereto as an independent person. (Civil Code Art. 15.). That the Civil Code places husband and wife on an equal footing, except when consideration for their common domestic life requires some modifications, may be seen from the provision of Art. 17, which allows a wife to do the acts above mentioned without the permission of her husband "when the interests of the husband and wife conflict," and also from the provision of Art. 790 in which it is stipulated that "a husband and wife are mutually bound to support and maintain each other."

The great revolution in the legal position of woman which the new Civil Code brought about is nowhere so clearly seen as in its regulations relating to the *property of married women.*

The laws relating to married women's property are different in different countries, and varies with the degree of civilization attained; but broadly, they may be grouped into the following *four systems*:—

(1) System of Conjugal Unity.—In those systems of law which regard man and wife as *one person*, or in which the wife's personality is merged in that of the husband, whatever the bride possesses at the time of marriage becomes the property of the busband, as was the case in the English Common Law, or under the doctrine of *Manus* in the early Roman Law, or that of *Mund* in the early Germanic Law.

(2) System of Dowry.—Another system sets aside a part, at least, of the bride's fortune as a common conjugal fund, the management of which belongs to the husband, as was the case at one period under Roman Law, and under the Code Civil, and as is now practiced in the South of France.

(3) System of General Community of Conjugal Property.— This system exists under the Code Civil side by side with the dotal system, principally in the northern part of

France.

(4) System of Separate Property.—Under this system marriage makes no change whatever in the property rights of the bride, as is the case in England since the Married Woman's Property Act of 1882, and in many States of the United States.

Broadly speaking, the usual process in the evolution of the law of conjugal property is in the order which I have stated above, the system of unity corresponding to the lowest, and the system of separate property to the highest, scale of civilization. But in this respect, the compilers of the new Code have taken a decided step, and leaped, at one bound, *from the system of complete merger of wife's property in that of the husband to the system of separate property*. According to the Code (Art. 793—807), persons who are about to marry are allowed to make any contract with regard to their connjugal property, which will be binding upon them and can be set up against a third person, if registered before the registration of the marriage. If such contract be not made between them, their relations in regard to property are governed by the general rules of conjugal property, which, among others, lays down the fundamental rule, that the property belonging to a wife at the time of marriage or acquired after marriage in her own name, shall be her separate property. (Civil Code Art. 807).

The reform in the Law of Divorce, which the new Civil Code made, also marks a great advance as regards the legal position of woman. During the second period, while the Japanese law belonged to the Chinese Family, the law of divorce was based upon the Chinese doctrine of "the Seven Grounds of Divorce" (七去) which are (1) sterility, (2) lewdness, (3) disobedience to father-in-law or mother-in-law, (4) loquacity, (5) larceny, (6) jealousy, and (7) bad disease. These grounds were adopted in the "House Law" (Koryō) of the Taihō Code.

But it must be observed that these grounds were *not lemitative*, as in the case of modern legislation. They are only mentioned as *just grounds for abandoning a wife*, or in some cases such as barrenness, adultery or hereditary disease, as a *moral obligation* which a husband owes to his ancestor to abandon the wife, because the object of marriage was the perpetuation of ancestor-worship, and barrenness may cause the failure of heir, adultery the confusion, and hereditary disease the pollution, of ancestral blood. (See my work on "Ancestorworship and Japanese Law"). Practically, a wife could be divorced at the pleasure of her husband, under any slight or flimsy pretext, the most usual being that "She does not conform to the usage of the family." It must be further observed that divorce during this period meant only the abandonment of the wife on the part of the husband. The wife had no legal right to demand divorce from her husband on any ground. Divorce, therefore, was not a bilateral, nor even a reciprocal, act. It was an *unilateral act of the husband.* To bring an action against the husband, or to give information of a crime against him was itself considered a grave offence; and so a wife could not demand divorce in the court of law. Divorce was the privilege of the husband only, as in the Mosaic and other primitive laws.

But this state of things has changed since the Japanese law passed from the Chinese and entered the European Family of Laws. In the 6th year of Meiji (1873) the following Law (No. 162) was enacted, which, for the first time, allowed the wife to bring an action of divorce against the husband:—"Whereas it has frequentry happened that a wife asked divorce from her husband on account of unavoidable circumstances, to which the latter unreasonably withheld his consent for many years, thereby causing her to lose the opportunity of second marriage, and whereas this is an injury to her right of freedom, it shall be henceforth allowed to the wife to bring an action against her husband, with the assistance of her father, brother or other relative." This law may be considered a revolution in the legal position of woman. The new Civil Code went a step farther and placed husband and wife on an equal footing in this respect. According to the Code *two kinds of divorce* are recognized, *consensual* and *judicial*, the former being effected by arrangement of parties, while the latter is granted by a court of law on several grounds specified in Art. 813 of the Code. The grounds for judicial divorce include, inter alia, bigamy, adultery, sentence for an offence of grave nature, such cruel treatment or gross insult as make living together unbearable, desertion with evil intent, cruel treatment or gross insult of or by lineal ascendant, uncertainty, for a period of three years or more, whether the consort is alive or dead. Consensual divorce requiring the *consent of both parties* is a bilateral act, whereas divorce during the second period was an *unilateral act*, which took place at the will of the husband who gave her a "letter of divorce" formulated, as a custom, in three lines and a half "mikudari-han," stating that he gave her a dismissal, and nothing should henceforth stand in the way of her marrying again. As to the judicial divorce, either party to marriage can claim divorce from the other, if any of the grounds specified by law exists, so that husband and wife are now placed on an equal footing in this respect.

It will appear from the foregoing rough sketch of the three periods in the history of the law relating to the position of woman, that during the first period, while Shintoism was the only form of worship, woman held a higher place than in the second period, when Confucianism, combined with Buddhism and Feudalism held down woman in a state of subjection; while in the third era, a great revolution has been made in the position of women, and equality with men as far as their private rights are concerned, is vouchsafed to them under the new Civil Codes.

X. The Status of Foreigners.

The possible forms, which the law of any country relating to the position of foreigners may assume, or the possible stages through which it may pass, may be arranged, by the broad generalization of comparative jurisprudence, under the *four* following heads :—

(1) Laws based upon the Principle of Enmity.

The laws of almost all barbarous peoples are based upon the principle that all foreigners are enemies, and consequently have no right whatever. Even after they cease to regard foreigners as enemies, they view their own laws as exclusively national, that is to say, they are applicable only to their own countrymen. Foreigners are, therefore, outlaws, and are placed outside the protection of the law.

(2) Laws based upon the Principle of Inferiority.

With the advance of civilization, especially with the progress of commerce, foreigners are no longer regarded as enemies, but from disdain for foreigners, or from national egoism, they are placed in inferior position as regards the enjoyment of their private rights. Sometimes the enjoyment of many rights is totally denied them, or sometimes capricious limitations are placed upon their legal capacities. In this stage, foreigners enjoy private rights, but in a limited degree only.

(3) Laws based upon the Principle of Reciprocity.

Some countries make the conditions of foreigners dependent upon the treatment which their own people receive in other countries ; and allow foreigners the enjoyment of their rights only so far as the countries of those foreigners allow their own people the same rights. This principle of reciprocity is adopted in France (Code Civil. Art. 11,), Austria (Das allg. buergerl, Gesetzbuch § 33.), Sweden, Norway, Servia and other countries.

(4) Laws based upon the Principle of Equality.

This is the most liberal and most advanced system of law relating to the legal condition of foreigners. Beginning in 1827 with the Dutch Civil Code, and followed by the Italian Civil Code of 1865, it has now been adopted in the majority of European and American States. They recognize the principle of equality as far as the enjoyment and exercise of private rights are concerned, some few exceptions only being usually made on grounds of national policy, such as the prohibition or limitation of the ownership of land or ships, the right of fishery, the right of working mines, or egaging in the coasting trade, and a few others.

Now, in regard to the legal condition of foreigners in Japan, we may distinguish *three periods*, which nearly correspond to the first, second and fourth stages above mentioned. The first period includes the time before the opening of the country to foreign intercourse; the second from that time until the new Civil Code came into operation; and the third from that time till the present day.

During the first period, which may be called the *Period of National Seclusion*, there was no intercourse with foreign countries. Foreigners were looked upon as barbarians or enemies. They could not come and reside in the country, except in a very few instances, and, therefore, they stood entirely outside the pale of the law.

The second period, which may be call *The period of the Treaties* begins from the date of the second visit of Commodore Perry in 1854 and the conclusion of the treaty of peace and amity by him, followed in 1858 by the first treaty of trade and commerce with the United States. Some ports were opened for foreign trade, and foreigners could come and reside within the limits of the treaty ports and engage in trade, business or missionary work. But their rights depended upon the *treaties, not upon the law of the country*. They enjoyed the privilege of extra-territoriality, that is to say, they brought their own laws with them, and remained under the jurisdiction of their respective consuls.

In the third period, which may be called the *Period of the Code*, foreigners enjoy their rights under the *law*, and the treaties only provide for the guarantees or limitations of rights. The new Civil Code, at its commencement, proclaims the noble principle of the equality of foreigners and native subjects before the law. Art. 2 provides that "Foreigners enjoy private rights except in those cases where such enjoyment is prohibited by law, ordinance or treaty." And as to foreign juridical persons, Art. 36 provides, that "The existence of jurisdical persons other than states, administrative districts and commercial companies, is not admitted. But foreign juridical persons recognized as such by law or treaty do not come under this rule.

Foreign juridical persons recognized as such under the provision of the preceding paragraph have the same private rights as the same classes of juridical persons existing in Japan; but this does not apply to such rights as foreigners cannot enjoy, or so far as special provisions are made by law or treaty."

From the above provisions, it will be seen that the *new Civil Code made the equal enjoyment of rights a general rule*, and limitations and prohibitions exceptions. These limitations upon the foreigner's equal enjoyment of rights are not numerous, and do not differ greatly from those existing under the laws of many other modern states. Such restrictions are the ownership of land or Japanese ships, the right to work mines, to own shares in the Bank of Japan or the Yokohama Specie Bank, to become members of the Stock Exchange, to engage in the emigration business, to receive bounties for navigation or ship-building and a few others. Otherwise foreigners are as free as the Japanese to engage in any commercial or industrial business, or to own shares in any Japanese companies. Even the restrictions above mentioned do not work so hard upon foreigners as it may at first appear, for, although foreigners as individuals can not own land, they may become members of any commercial company owning land or working mines. As individuals, they may have the right of superficies which is the right to use another person's land for the purpose of enjoying the right of property in structures and trees thereon. Moreover, the Law No. 39 of 1901, a right *in rem* called "the right of perpetual lease" was created especially for the benefit of foreigners or foreign juridical persons, who had held land in the treaty ports under lease from the Japanese government. These leases which had been no more than rights *in personam* were turned into rights *in rem*, and *the rules relating to ownership are applied to them.* So, they are now practically the same as ownership; and as soon as they pass into the hands of Japanese subjects they are turned into ownership. Moreover, opinions in favour of allowing foreigners to own land are daily gaining strength, so that this restriction is quite likely to be removed ere long.

It will appear from the foregoing statement that the condition of foreigners has undergone a great revolution during the half century which elapsed since the opening of the country. In the *first period*, foreigners had *no right* whatever; in the *second period*, they enjoyed their private rights *under treaties*; but in the *third period*, that is, under the new Civil Code, they enjoy their private rights *under the law*, which recognizes the principle of *equality* as far as private rights are concerned. Thus, in a comparatively short space of time, *Japanese law passed from the stage of Enmity to that of Equality*—a revolution, which, in other countries, required many centuries to accomplish. The difference between the second stage in which their enjoyment of rights depended upon treaties, and the third stage in which their rights depend upon law, very clearly appears in the present condition of Russians in Japan. As the commercial treaties between

Japan and Russia have come to an end by the outbreak of the war, if Russian subjects had enjoyed their rights only under the treaties, they would not be entitled to claim any protection from Japan, except as a matter of favour. But as their rights are now guaranteed by the provisions of the Code, Russian residents still remaining in Japan enjoy the protection of law, just as peacefully as the citizens of any friendly states. The Code assures them the equal enjoyment of private rights, whether the country to which they belong be in amicable relations with Japan or not. This difference is further illustrated by Imperial Ordinance No. 352 of 1899, which declared foreigners who are not citizens of any of the Treaty Powers to have equal freedom of residence and profession with the subjects of the treaty Powers.

XI. The House and Kinship.

It will be at once remarked by any one reading the new Civil Code that the Japanese family law, unlike that of Europe and America, rests upon the *double bases of House and Kinship.* The House or "iye," in the sense in which it is employed in the Japanese law, does not mean a household, nor a dwelling place, but a group of persons, bearing the same surname, and subject to the authority of its chief who is called "Koshu" or House-head. The other members who are subject to the authority of the house-head are called "Kazoku" or House-members. It is not necessary that a house should consist of a group of persons, for a house may exist even when there is only one person in it, in which case that person is still called "Koshu" or house-head. The house-membership consists of those relatives of the house-head or his predecessors, or sometimes also, of the relatives of house-members who are not related to the present or preceding house-heads by any tie of kinship, but who entered the house with the house-head's consent; such for instance, as the relatives of the house-head's adopted son, or daughter-in-law. (Civil Code. Art. 732—745) The persons who constitute the members of a house are defined by law, and a registry is kept, in each district, of persons who are in each house. The house-membership is constituted in accordance with the following rules.

1. A child enters the house of its father.
2. A child whose father is not known enters the house of its mother.
3. A "Shoshi" or natural born child recognized by its father who is a house-member, or a natural-born child of a female member of a house enters the house of its father or mother, only when the house-head's consent is obtained.
4. A wife enters the house of her husband, except when a female house-head contracts a marriage, in which case the husband enters the house of his wife.
5. A relative of a house-head who is in another house or a relative of a house-member who has become such by adoption or marriage, enters the house, if the consent of the head, both of the house he is leaving, and of the house he is entering, is obtained. A person who cannot enter any house, such as a child whose parents can not be ascertained, establishes a new house, and becomes himself a house-head.

A house thus constituted is entered in the House-registry or "Koseki" which is kept in every district throughout the Empire.

Kinship, according to the Civil Code arises from relationship by blood, by adoption or by marriage, and exists

1. Between relatives by blood within six degrees inclusive.
2. Between husband and wife.
3. Between relatives by marriage within three degrees inclusive. (Civil Code. Art. 725).
4. Between an adopted child and adoptive parent and the

latter's blood-relatives, the same relationship exists, from the date of the adoption, as that between blood relatives. (Civil Code. Art. 727).

5. Between step-parents and step-children, a wife and her husband's recognized child, the same relationship exists as that between parent and child.

Now, a house may include persons who are not the kindred of the house-head, because it includes the kindred of the preceding house-head, or the kindred of a house-member who is not related to the present house-head; and may exclude even the nearest kindred, because, by adoption or marriage and other causes above mentioned, a man may enter another house, or return to the original house by the dissolution of the marriage or adoptive tie, or establish a new house, leaving his own parents or child in the original house. The *house, therefore, is wider than kinship on the one side, whilst it is narrower on the other.* Sir Henry Maine's description of the ancient family so well tallys with the present state of the house in Japanese law—except in one particular which shows the peculiarity of Japanese family law,—that I cannot do better than quote his words in full.

"The family, then, is the type of an archaic society in all the modifications which it was capable of assuming; but the family here spoken of is not exactly the family as understood by a modern. In order to reach the ancient conception, we must give to our modern ideas an important extension and an important limitation. We must look on the family as constantly enlarged by the absorption of strangers within its circle, and we must try to regard the fiction of adoption as so closely simulating the reality of kinship that neither law nor opinion makes the slightest difference between a real and an adoptive connexion. On the other hand, the persons theoretically amalgamated into a family by their common descent are practically held together by common obedience to their highest living ascendant, the father, grandfather, or great-grandfather. The patriarchal authority of a chieftain is as necessary an ingredient in the notion of the family group as the fact (or assumed fact) of its having sprung from his loins; and hence we must understand that if there be any persons who, however truly included in the brotherhood by virtue of their blood-relationship, have nevertheless *de facto* withdrawn themselves from the empire of its ruler, they are always, in the beginnings of law, considered as lost to the family. It is this patriarchal aggregate—the modern family thus cut down on one side and extended on the other—which meets us on the threshold of primitive jurisprudence." (Maine, Ancient Law, ch. V.)

Here I may conveniently compare the House in Japanese law with the Family in Roman Law, in order to show the characteristics of the former. It differs from the Roman family chiefly in the following points:—

(1) The House is not a family-group held together by "common obediênce to the *highest living ascendant*" as in the Roman family, but is a *legal entity originally founded on ancestor-worship*. Therefore, it would be nearer the truth to say that it is the *highest dead ascendant*, by the common obedience to whom a house is held together. The house-head is not necessarily the highest living ascendant, but is a person who *succeeds to the authority* of the highest ascendant. Sometimes, therefore, a son may be the house-head, and his father may be a house-member under his authority, as in the case of abdication of the house-headship, which I will explain presently. Or, sometimes, a nephew may be the house-head, and the uncle may be a house-member under him, as will happen, when a grandson succeeds to the grandfather by representation. Or again, there may be no relationship at all between the house-head and the house-member as I have explained above.

(2) In consequence of the above difference, the Roman family dissolved at the *death* of each paterfamilias, and each of the next highest ascendants became in his turn *sui juris* and a paterfamilias, having all his descendants in his power. Thus, if the deceased paterfamilias had three sons, there would be three families instead of one. But the Japanese house is never dissolved at the death or abdication of a house-head and is succeeded by one person, all other members remaining *alieni juris* as before.

(3) According to the present Japanese law, *a woman may become a house-head*, and if she marries, she may continue to be the house-head and have her husband as a house-member under her power, provided such intention is expressed at the time of the marriage. (Civil Code. Art. 736.) Under Roman Law, however, a woman could never exercise authority even over her children.

(4) According to Roman Law, when a woman married, she always entered the husband's family and passed into the power of another; but according to Japanese law the *husband enters the house of his wife* in case of the marriage of a female house-head, and also in case of the adoption of a son-in-law or "muko-yōshi," which I will explain later on; so that the famous maxim of Roman Law "*Mulier est caput et finis familiae*"—a woman is the beginning and end of the family—does not apply to Japanese.

(5) Patria potestas was among the Romans an institution of *private law;* and it is so with us at the present time. But before the Restoration, it was an institution of public law as well as of private law, as I will explain when I come to speak of the decay of the house-system.

XII. House-Headship and Parental Power.

From the nature of the double bases of the Japanese Family Law, it follows that *a person may have two capacities*, one as a member of the legal house, and the other as a member of the wider group of kindred. Thus, a person may be a house-head or a house-member, and, at the same time, he may be a son. In such cases, if he is the son of a house-head, he is placed under the house-head's power and under the parental power of the same person; if he is a son of a house-member, who is himself under the power of the house-head, he is under the power of two persons, the house-head and the father. But if the house-head is a minor, and his father or mother is a house-member, the former is under the parental power of the latter, while the latter is subject to the authority of the former. In such cases, conflict or inconvenience which may arise from mutual subjection to one another, is avoided by the provision of Art. 895 of the Civil Code, according to which the parent exercises the house-head's power on behalf of the minor house-head.

Of the two bases of the Japanese Family Law, the House and the Kindred, *more weight is always laid on the former than on the latter*, except in the two instances of the duties of support and maintenance and the succession to the property of house-members, both of which are new institutions introduced by the Code and are not bound by the limit of the house. In most other cases, the house takes precedence of the kindred, and a man's rights and duties, capacities and incapacities are usually determined by his position as a member of the house, and not by his position as a member of the kindred. *Parental power* which is based on the conception of kinship *is limited by the concep-*

tion of the house, and is recognized only so far as the parent and child are in the same house. So, if a son is not in the same house with his father or mother, he does not stand under the paternal power of either. The consent of the house-head is always necessary for the marriage, adoption, divorce or the dissolution of adoption of the house-member, but the consent of parents is only required *when the offspring is in the same house with them.*

Here again appears the difference between the Roman and Japanese family laws. The former recognizes only one authority of the head of the family, in the *patria potestas* of the highest male ascendant, and merged the parental power of the members of the family in that of the paterfamilias, while the Japanese law recognizes parental authority of the house-member side by side with the authority of the house-head. The authority of the house-head includes the right of consent above referred to, right of determining the residence of house-members, right of expelling them from the house or forbidding their return to it on certain grounds specified by law, and the right of succeeding to the house-member's property in default of other heirs. The parental power includes the custody and education of children who are minors, right of correction, right of determining their place of abode, business or profession, of managing their property, or performing several legal acts on their behalf, subject in some cases to the approval of a family council. Most of the right falling under the parental power *were formerly included in the house-head's power*, but the new Civil Code recognized the authority of parent and transferred them to the parental power, and greatly curtailed that of the house-head, only leaving those rights to him, which are necessary to the preservation and proper management of the house. This recognition by the Civil Code of the parental power beside the authority of the house-head shows the transient state of Japanese society and is one of the points regarding which the framers of the new Code took pains to adjust the laws to the progressive tendencies of the society. Formerly, there was only one authority recognized by Japanese law, as in the case of Roman Law—that of the house-head. But the new Civil Code took a decided step and recognized the parental power, besides the house-headship, due allowance being made to the long-existing custom among the people, by not going so far as to extend that recognition to the parents who belong to a different house from that of the child. The tendency of the laws of a progressive society must be the *gradual recognition of natural relationship in place of artificial connections*; and the process of evolution in this branch of law is *from House to Kinship*. The reform made by the new Civil Code may be regarded as the first step in that direction.

XIII. Relationships.

The method of determining the degrees of relationship according to the new Civil Code is the same as that adopted in most countries of Europe and America, belonging to the system of Roman Law; that is, by reckoning the number of generations which intervene between two persons, either directly when they are lineal relatives, or through a common ancestor, when they are collaterals. This system of determining the degrees of relationship by the distance of consanguinity is the most natural one and is, for that reason, adopted from Western jurisprudence by the framers of the Code. But, previous to the adoption of the Code, while Japanese law still belonged to the Family of Chinese Law, relationship was determined in a different way. The basis of the new system is *the distance of blood-relationship* between relatives; but the old law rested on the *double bases of blood-relationship and family rank*, that is to say, the degree of relationship was determined not only by the distance of blood-relationship, real or fictitious, but also by the consideration of *superiority* or *inferiority* of their relative positions in the family. In " the Ceremony Law " of the Taihō Code (701 A. D.), kindred are divided into the following Five Ranks or " Go-tō-shin."

(1) The Relatives of First Rank are; father and mother, adoptive father and adoptive mother, husband, son and daughter.

(2) The Relatives of the Second Rank are; grandfather and grandmother, " tekibo " (or wife of the father of a concubine's child), step-mother, uncle and aunt, brothers and sisters, husband's parents, wife and concubine, brother's child, grandson and granddaughter, and son's wife.

(3) The Relatives of the Third Rank are; great grandfather and great grandmother, uncle's wife, husband's nephew, cousin, brother and sister by half-blood on father's side, husband's grandfather and grandmother, husband's uncle and aunt, wife of nephew, step-father, and child of husband by his former wife or concubine, provided the child is living in the same house.

(4) The Relatives of the Fourth Rank are; great great grandfather and great great grandmother, grandfather's brother and sister, father's cousin, husband's brother and sister, brother's wife and concubine, second consin, grandfather and grandmother on mother's side, uncle and aunt on mother's side, brother's grandchild, cousin german's child, sister's child, great grandchild, grandson's wife and concubine and child of wife's or concubine's former consort.

(5) The Relatives of the Fifth Rank are; parents of wife or concubine, aunt's child, cousin on mother's side, great great grandchild, grandchild by a daughter who entered another house by marriage, and son-in-law.

The above table will show that the degree of relationship was greatly modified by the consideration of rank in the family; so that those who stand in the same rank are not always related in an equal degree, when measured only with reference to the distance of consanguinity. It will be seen that *precedence is generally given to father's and husband's relatives, and to those who are in the same house, in preference to mother's and wife's relatives and to those who are in another house.* Thus, uncle and aunt on the father's side stand in the Second Rank, while those on the mother's side stand in the Fourth. Husband is the relative of the First Rank to wife, but the wife is the relative of the Second Rank to the husband. Husband's parents are in the Second Rank, while wife's parents are in the Fifth. Nephew and niece by brother are in the Second Rank, while those by sister are in the Fourth. Grandchild by son is in the Second, while grandchild by daughter is in the Fifth Rank, because the latter is in another house on account of marriage.

The law also made distinction between " sonzoku " or " superior kin" and "hizoku" or "inferior kin." The former includes all relatives, lineal and collateral, who stand above any person in the same lateral line of the table of consanguinity; such as father, uncle, father's cousin, grandfather etc, while the latter includes those who stand in the lateral lines below him, such as son, nephew, cousin's child, grandson etc.

This system of classifying relatives into Five Ranks was derived from the *Chinese Law of Mourning.* From ancient times down to the present day, Chinese law has been very strict as to mourning, because it was considered as the highest duty of a man to show respect and love toward the departed soul of his relative by that act; and the moral as well as the legal code prescribed even the " Mourning of Three Years " to the dutiful son. Chinese codes abound in minute regulations as to the mourning dress, the duration of the time of mourning and the conduct of mourners. The *mourning dress is divided into five classes* and the duration of the period of mourning is fixed by the class of the mourning dress which the mourner ought to wear. The mourning dress is coarser in material and make, as the person mourned for stands nearer and higher in the family position to the mourner ; the first class which is worn for parents, husband, and husband's parents, being the coarsest. The first class mourning dress is worn for three years, the second for two years, the third, for nine months, the fourth for five months and the fifth for three months. Relatives are classified *according to the five classes of mourning dresses* which are worn for them. Thus, for instance father and mother belong to the relative of the first class mourning dress ; grandparents to the second class ; cousins to the third ; great uncles and aunts to the fourth ; and wife's parents to the fifth. This *classification of relatives according to the five classes of mourning dresses very nearly corresponds to the Five Ranks mentioned in the Taihō Code*, except with respect to great grandparents who belong to the Third and Fourth Rank respectively according to the Taihō Code, but who are placed according to Chinese law in the second class. Besides, this classification which is made in the Ceremonial Law of the Chinese Codes, finds its place in the "Ceremony Law" or "Gi-sei-ryō" of the Taihō Code, instead of the "House Law" where one would naturally expect to find it. So, there is little room for doubt, that the above-mentioned *Japanese classification of the relatives into the "Five Ranks" had its origin in the Chinese law of mourning dress.*

During the Tokugawa Shogunate, the study of the Chinese classics was greatly encouraged, and in 1638 the famous "Mourning Law" (服忌令) was made, which has since then been amended several times and the classification of the "Five Ranks" went practically into disuse, until it was revived by the Criminal Code of 1870, which struck off concubines from the Third, Fourth and Fifth Ranks, and made a few other unimportant alterations. But with the publication of the present Criminal Code in 1882, it was abolished, and was replaced sixteen years later, by the present system of reckoning relationship adopted in the new Civil Code. In this respect too, Japanese law has passed from the Chinese to the European Family of Law.

XIV. The Law of Personal Registration and the Civil Code.

As the house in the Japanese Family Law is narrower, in one respect, than kindred, and may exclude even the nearest relatives by blood, and wider, in another respect, and may include strangers, there is no logical test to determine the sphere of persons constituting the house other than their common subjection to the authority of one man, the house-head. Some other *external legal evidence* is required, therefore, for determining the constituent of a particular house. Such evidence is supplied by the *register* which is kept in every district throughout the Empire. As a person's birth, marriage, adoption, guardianship, death, succession, entrance to, or separation from, a house, acquisition or loss of nationality, and every other change of man's status is recorded in the register, the law relating to registration forms a supplementary law to the Civil Code and the present law was promulgated and put into force on the same day as the Code. As the register is the record of man's legal position in society, the development of society is often reflected in the law of registration. *Three stages* may be distinguished in the history of the law of personal registration in Japan; 1st, the *Epoch of Clan-registration*, 2nd, the *Epoch of House-registration*, and 3rd, the *Epoch of Status-registration*. These epochs show the changes in the units of state and correspond to the three stages in the process of social disintegration.

In the early days of Japanese history, it was not the individual nor the family that formed the unit of state. The state only took cognizance of *clans* and the government of families and individuals in each clan was left to the chief of the clan or "uji-no-kami" who was usually the eldest male descendant of an eponymous ancestor. He was honored and obeyed by clansmen as the representative of their common ancestor. He was the head of their worship, their leader in time of war, and their governor in time of peace. There were Great Clans or "ō-uji" and Small Clans or "ko-uji," the latter being included in the former. Clansmen of the Small Clan were governed by their chief who was himself subject to the chief of the Great Clan. The Emperor was the supreme authority over them, and all the laws and proclamations of the Imperial Government were transmitted to the "uji-no-kami" of the Great Clans, who, in turn, transmitted them to the "uji-no-kami" of the Small Clans. Thus each clan was a body founded on community of blood and worship and *formed an administrative division of the country*, corresponding to the present administrative divisions, such as provinces, cities, towns, district and villages.

Since the introduction of Chinese civilization and the Reform of the Taika Era (645 A. D.), in spite of the fact that the clan-system of government continued for a long time afterward, the basis of the administrative division of the country gradually changed from a *personal* to a *territorial system* and provinces and districts took the place of clans.

In those early days of clan-government, it was of the utmost importance that each man's clan-name should be kept sacred. As only those who belonged to certain clans could fill high official positions, or join the Imperial body-guard, and as several other privileges were enjoyed by particular clans, attempts were often made by clansmen to forsake their original clans and surreptitiously adopt the names of other and more iufluential clans. In order to put a stop to these abuses, the "ordeal of hot-water" or "kugadachi" was resorted to, which consisted in plunging the hand into hot water before the temple of a god. It was claimed that those who assumed false clan-names would suffer injury, while the innocent would escape unhurt. Afterward, in the year 815 A. D., a "Register of Clan-names" or "Seishi-roku" was compiled, a part of which is still in existence to-day. This Register consisted of 30 volumes and contained 1182 clan-names.

The introduction of the House-register or "ko-seki" dates back as far as the 1st year of the Taika Era. But it owes its origin to the adoption of Chinese institutions, and although its introduction was earlier in date than the final compilation of the register of clan-names, its historical order must come after that of the Clan-Registry, for the system of House-Registry has continued from that remote period down to the present time.

It was only in the year of the publication of the new Civil Code (1898), that our law of registration began to enter upon the third stage of its development. The present law, which was promulgated at the same time as the Civil Code, and which replaced the previous law of 1871 still retains the name of "Koseki Hō" or the "Law of House-Registration;" but *the character of the law has undergone a change*, necessitated by the progress of the social condition of the country, for it provides for the *registration of individual status or "mibun-tōki" as well as of house registration.*

It is sometimes asserted that the family was the original unit of the state, and that an aggregation of families formed a clan. But *this view seems to reverse the real order of development.* The clan grew out of the expansion of a family, and separate households grew np within the clan by the increase of clansmen. It was their common worship and common clan-name which united them to a group. So it was the clan which was first recognized by the state and formed its unit. The family or house was included in the clan and did not yet possess separate existence in the eyes of the law. It *was only by the gradual disintegration of the clan and the growth of the central power of the state that the family or house came to the fore, and began to form the unit of the state. Thus, the constituent elements of each society become smaller and smaller, until they divide themselves into atoms or individuals.*

XV. Adoption.

The importance of the fiction of adoption to primitive society has been illustrated by Sir Henry Maine in many places. In one passage, he says, " Without the fiction of Adoption which permits the family tie to be artificially created, it is difficult to understand how society would ever have escaped from its swaddling-clothes, and taken its first step towards civilization " (Ancient Law ch. II.) Its importance in India and also at Rome and Athens is well known among students of historical and comparative jurisprudence. But in modern systems of law, adoption no longer occupies the position of importance which it held in archaic societies. It still survives in most of the countries which have received Roman Law, but with several restrictions as to its effects, which make it in no way resemble that assumption of real kinship which characterized the ancient form of adoption. To the English Family of Law, it is totally unknown as a legal institution.

But in Japan, adoption may be regarded as the corner-stone of Family Law. Without it, the continuity of the House, upon which rests the perpetuation of ancestor-worship, cannot be maintained. The practice of adoption has been so common and universal among the people, from ancient time down to the present day, that Prof. Chamberlain writes "It is strange, but true, that you may often go into a Japanese family and find half-a-dozen persons calling each other parent and child, brother and sister, uncle and nephew, and yet being really either no blood-relations at all, or else relations in quite different degrees from those conventionally assumed."

Adoption in different systems of law *may be classified with regard to its object, under the following four heads* :—

(1) Adoption for the purpose of pertetuating the family *sacra*.

(2) Adoption for the purpose of obtaining a *successor to house-headship*.

(3) Adoption for the purpose of obtaining a *successor to property*.

(4) Adoption for *charitable purposes, or for consolation in case of childless marriage*.

The historical order of the developement, or rather the decay, of the law of adoption is usually as indicated above. I will proceed to explain them in order.

(1) Adoption for the purpose of perpetuating Family sacra.

Death without an heir to perpetuate the worship of ancestors was considered to be the greatest act of impiety which a descendant could commit. So, in the case of the failure of male issue, it was the *bounden duty* of a house-head to acquire a son by means of adoption. Adoption was, as Fustel de Coulanges says, "a final resource to escape the much dreaded misfortune of the extinction of a worship."

Many provisions of our ancient Code show that the object of adoption was the perpetuation of the sacra. The House Law of the Taihō Code provides that "A person *having no child* may adopt one from among his relatives *within the Fourth Rank of Kinship*, whose age does not exceed that which might have been attained by a son of the adoptor's own body." According to some commentators on the Taihō Code, " having no child " here means that the adoptive father should have reached the age of *sixty* years, or the adoptive mother *fifty* years, without having *male issue*. The reason for *limiting the age of the adoptor* was, that as long as any hope of having a male issue of blood, that is, the direct descendant of his ancestors, existed, the head of a house should not permit a person of more distant relationship to become the successor to the sacra.

That the object of adoption was the perpetuation of ancestor-worship may also be inferred from the old strict rule that only a *kinsman could be adopted as a son*. The Taihō Code did not permit adoption of kindred beyond the *Fourth Rank*, as I have said above. From the remains of the Taihō Criminal Code which have come down to us, we know that a punishment of one year's penal servitude was inflicted upon one who adopted a son from a different clan. This prohibition against the adoption of a person not related by blood derives its origin from the belief which generally exists where the practice of ancestor-worship prevails, that " *the spirit does not receive the offerings of strangers*."

Another requirement of adoption, which is to be found in the laws of many countries, is the absolute *failure of male issue*. The House Law of the Taihō Code allowed adoption only in case a man had no son. The object of this rule is clear from what I have said above. A remoter relative should not be admitted where there is a nearer descendant to make offerings.

There is one peculiar form of adoption called " muko-yōshi " or " adoption of son-in-law," the origin of which must be attributed to the same cause. As I have said above, the law considered a man *childless*, even though he had a daughter. Males were the only continuators of worship. Those who had daughters only were, therefore, obliged to adopt a son; but it was necessary for the blood of the ancestor to be, if possible, *contin-*

ned in the house. In such cases, a house-head selects a person who is fit to be his daughter's husband and adopts him as a son. If adoption and marriage take place at the same time, it is called "muko-yōshi" or "adoption of son-in-law." The same object may also be attained by the subsequent marriage of the adopted son with the daughter of the adoptor, for the collateral relationship of brother and sister *by adoption* is no bar to their marriage.

(2) Adoption for the purpose of obtaining a successor to House-headship.

As the house is the seat of ancestor-worship and the house-head is the continuator of the sacra, this kind of adoption cannot be regarded as differing from that above mentioned. But with the development of the house-system, the authority of the head of a house begins to be regarded as a distinct object of inheritance by itself and the family sacra only as one of the duties incumbent upon the house-head. Especially was this the case, when hereditary office, profession or fief belonged to house-headship. In Japan, this stage was reached when the Feudal System was established, and Daimios and Samurais had their fiefs belonging to their houses Under the Feudal régime, *the nature of military service required that males only should become house-heads.* Hence the failure of male issue was also the cause of adoption. It was necessary to make provision against the continzency of a house becoming extinct and the fief being escheated by failure of heirs. As professions were at that time usually hereditary and were considered as belonging to certain houses, adoption was frequently resorted to, in order to keep the profession in the house. Physicians, artists, masters of fencing, riding, archery, professors of classics and the like often adopted, by special permission, those qualified to succeed them in the profession, even though they may have had sons of their own, the latter, however, being unworthy of their fathers. This kind of adoption was called " geidō-yōshi " or " arts-adoption."

It has just been remarked that the Taihō Code fixed the lower limit of the adoptor's age at sixty for the father and fifty for the mother. But this rule took another form under the law of the Tokugawa Government. The limit of the age was fixed as low as *seventeen*. A house-head above that age, or even by special permission under that age, who had no male issue was allowed to adopt a son, in order to prevent the extinction of a house by his sudden death, causing the escheat of his feudal property. A person between the ages of seventeen and fifty years could even adopt a son on his death-bed, which kind of adoption was called "kiu-yōshi" or "quick adoption." But after the age of fifty, "quick adoption" was not allowed, so that he was obliged to provide for the succession to the house-headship early in life, even if he still had the hope of having male issue. The Taihō Code allowed adoption only in old age, because it was desirable that ancestor-worship should be continued by the nearest blood descendants. The Tokugawa Law allowed and encouraged adoption by young people, and attached severe penalties to the neglect of the precaution to provide for succession early in life, in order to avoid the chance of a house becoming extinct.

(3) Adoption for the purpose of obtaining a successor to Property.

Next comes the time when the notions of succession to sacra and house-headship gradually recede into the background and the notion of property succession comes to the fore. This stage is first reached in the new Civil Code. With the Restoration of the Imperial power and the abolition of Feudalism, house-headship has lost more than half of its former importance. Fiefs were abolished; offices and professions ceased to be hereditary privileges of house-heads; and, so far as public law is concerned, house-members now stand on an equal footing with house-heads. What remains of the rights and privileges attaching to house-heads is enjoyed within the sphere of private law. Of these the right of enjoying house-property is the most important, at least, so far as material interests are concerned. Besides, housemembers are now allowed to have independent property of their own, as I have already explained, and they may adopt just in the same way as house-heads, provided the consent of the latter is obtained. (Civil Code. Art. 750). During the Feudal period, only house-heads were allowed to adopt, because the object of adoption was the continuation of house-headship; but now *adoption is no longer the exclusive privilege of house-heads* because its object is not limited to obtaining a successor to house-headship. Wills, although not quite unknown to the old Japanese law, were very rare in practice and their place was taken by adoption. *What is done in Europe and America by will is done in Japan by adoption.* Instead of giving away property to another person by will, which becomes effective after death, a Japanese takes another person into his house by adoption during his lifetime and makes the latter the expectant successor to his property.

(4) Adoption for Consolation in case of Childless Marriage.

This is the only kind of adoption which has no connection with the house-system and marks the last stage in the history of the law of adoption. In Occidental systems of jurisprudence, will has taken the place of adoption, and the principal ground on which this institution is still retained is for consolation in case of childless marriage. Although the adopted child usually obtains the right of succeeding to the adoptor's property, this is the effect of adoption and cannot be regarded as the ground for allowing adoption. Consolation in the case of a childless marriage constitutes the principal motive to this act, and therefore most systems allow adoption only when the adoptor has no children of his own and is of such an age as to preclude reasonable expectation of any being born to him. In Japan also adoption often takes place from the same motive, but it cannot be regarded as a legal ground, because the new Civil Code does not limit adoption to the case of childless marriage. The Japanese law of adoption is now in a transient state, and *is passing from the second to the third stage of its development, but has not yet entered the fourth.*

XVI. Succession in General.—The Evolution of the Law of Succession.

I think it may be laid down as an universal rule of the evolution of the law of succession that it passes throgh *three stages of evolution;* the *fist stage is that of the succession to sacra,* the *second that of the succession to status* and the *third that of the successsion to property.* Each stage of development, however, did not form a distinct period in itself, but the later was gradually evolved out of the earlier by the process of differentation. In ancient times, the duty of performing and continuing the *worship* rested on the head of a house, and the property of a house belonged exclusively to him. He exercised *authority* over the members of his house, because he was the *continuator of the ancestral sacra,* and, in one sense, the representative of the ancestor. He owned his property, because it was left by the ancestor, and the *authority and property of a house-head rested on the worship of ancestors.* In those times, continuation of house-worship formed the sole object of inheritance. But in the course of time, the authority of the house-head which at first comprehended both power over the members of the house and rights over house property, came to be considered by itself in law. Afterwards the two constituent elements of the authority of the house-head gradually began to be separately considered, until, at last, *property came to be regarded as a distinct object of inheritance.*

There are perhaps few systems of law which can illustrate the above proposition and indicate the process of gradual development so clearly as the Japanese law of succession to the headship of a house. In the Succession Law "Keishi-ryo" of the Taihō-Code (701 A.D.) there is a provision that if a presumptive heir of a noble family "is not fit to succeed to the important duty" owing to the committal of crime or to disease, he may be disinherited and another presumptive heir may be substituted. The official commentary on this Code "Ryō-no-gigé" says "*to succeed to the important duty*" means "to suceeed a father and *inherit the sacra*, for the matter of worship is the most important." It appears that, at this time, the continuation of ancestor-worship was the principal object of succession. Since the middle ages, the word "*Katoku Sozoku*" or "the succession to house-authority" was used for succession, and in the Feudal period, espesially during the Tokugawa Shōgunate, succession represented the continuity of the *status of house-headship*. In later times "Katoku" which literally means "*house-authority*" was very frequently used for "*house-property*" which formed the object of inheritance just as the word "familia" in Roman law was often used to designate property. This transition of the use of the word "Katoku" indicates that the law of succession was gradually passing from the second to the third stage referred to.

The present law of succession, contained in Book V of the Civil Code, shows that *Japanese law is rapidly passing from the second to the third stage above mentioned, without losing its original trait of the succession to sacra.* The new Civil Code recognizes *two kinds* of succession; *Succession to house-headship* or "katoku sōzoku" and *Succession to property* or "isan sōzoku." But there are many rules still remaining, which show that the foundation of the succession to the house-headship is the necessity of continuing the worship of ancestors. Article 987 contains the following provision:—

"The ownership of the records of the genealogy of the house, the article used for house-worship and the family tombs constitutes the special right of succession to the headship of a house."

This important provision means that those things which are specified therein form the special objects of inheritance. They cannot be bequeathed away, nor can they be seized for debts.

Though the house is no longer a corporation, as was formerly the case, it is still a legal entity whose continuance is assured by law, and does not break up at the death of each house-head. So, there can be only one heir to its headship, and the new Civil Code recognizes many kinds of heirs to house-headship in order to provide against the contingency of the failure of the heir. They are; 1st, "the Legal Heir," 2nd, "the Appointed Heir," 3rd, "the Chosen Heir" and 4th, "the Ascendant Heir." The Legal Heir who comes first in the order of succession, *is the lineal descendant of a house-head, who is at the same time a member of his house.* Among lineal descendants, nearest kinsmen are preferred to more remote, males to females, and legetimate children to illegitimate, seniors in age being always accorded priority when they are equal in other respects (Civil Code. Art. 970). Modern writers on law usually give as a reason for the preference of nearer to remoter kinsmen that the order of succession is determined by the *degree of affection* which the deceased is presumed to have entertained towards his relatives, and also by the presumed intention of the person who dies intestate as to the disposition of his property. For the preference of males over females *feudal reasons* are often given. These reasons also form the principal basis of our present law. But, the reasons for the *existence* of the rule and its *origin* are not always the same. Originally, the *nearest in blood to the ancestors worshipped*, and their male descendants were preferred, because they were considered to be the fittest persons to offer sacrifices to the spirits of ancestors.

The Legal Heir is *heres necessarius* and is not allowed to renounce the succession, whilst other kinds of heirs are at liberty to accept or renounce the inheritance, or to accept it with the reservation, that they shall not be liable for the debts of their predecessors. It is the bounden duty of a descendant who is the Legal Heir to accept the inheritance and continue the sacra of the house.

The house-head cannot bequeath away from him more than one half of the property (Civil Code. Art. 1130), nor can he disinherit him, unless there exists one of the grounds mentioned in Article 975 of the Civil Code. The causes especially mentioned there are:—

(1) ill-treatment or gross insult to the house-head, (2) unfitness for house-headship on account of bodily or mental infirmities, (3) sentence to punishment for an offence of a nature disgraceful to the name of the house and (4) interdiction as a spendthrift. These grounds relate directly to the house-head's authority and indirectly to ancestor-worship and the necessity of maintaining intact the reputation and property of the house.

In case there is no legal presumptive heir to a house-head, he may appoint an heir, either in his lifetime or by his will. (Civil Code. Art. 979).

If, at the time of the death of a house-head, there is neither a Legal Heir, nor an Appointed Heir, the father of the deceased, or if there is no father, or if he is unable to express his intention, the mother, or, if there are no parents or both are unable to express their intention, the family council chooses an heir from among the members of the house according to the following order:—1st, the surviving wife, if she is a "*house-daughter*," 2nd, brothers, 3rd, sisters, 4th, the surviving wife who *is not a house-daughter*, and finally 5th, the lineal descendants of brothers and sisters (Civil Code. Art. 982).

Now, in this also, the desire for preserving the blood of ancestors will be seen from the order in which the heir is chosen. The surviving consort of the last house-head comes *first* in the order of succession, provided that she is a "*house-daughter*," but *fourth* if she is not the descendant in blood of an ancestor of the house.

If there is neither a Legal, nor Appointed, nor Chosen Heir, then the nearest lineal ascendant of the last house-head succeeds, males being always preferred to females between persons standing in the same degree of relationship (Civil Code. Art. 984).

If there are no other heirs above mentioned, the family council must choose one from among other relatives of the last house-head or members of his house, house-heads of branch-house or members of principal or branch-house. If none of the presons above mentioned be existing or able to succeed, then as a last resort, the family council may choose an heir from among other persons (Civil Code. Art. 985).

From the foregoing enumeration of the various kinds of heirs, it will be seen that the law takes every precaution against the contingency of a house becoming extinct; for with the extinction of the house, the worship of its ancestors would come to an end.

XVII. Property Succession.—The Recognition of House-member's Separate Property.

The second kind of succession, namely Property Succession is a new institution introduced by the new Civil Code. According to the Code, *Property Succession includes only the succession to the property of a house-member on his death.*

Before the Restoration, a house was in a strict sense a corporation, and a house-member could not have separate property of his own. All he gained he gained for the house-head or rather the house; all he possessed or enjoyed he possessed or enjoyed by the license of the house-head, not as of right. No question of succession to the property of house-members could therefore arise at that time. But the Restoration completely changed this state of things. It was one of the policies of the new Imperial Government to appoint its officials not, as before, on account of birth, but on account of personal merits, no distinction whatever being made as to whether they were house-heads or house-members. Fomerly, it was only the house-head that could hold public office. During the first years of the Imperial Government, statesmen and soldiers who had served in the cause of the Restoration were rewarded with life or perpetual annuities. But many of them were not house-heads; some were "inkyo" or house-members who had become such by abdicating house-headship, others were younger members of houses. Now, *these annuities and the salaries of civil and military officials being given by the State for personal services or merits, could not be treated as house-property. Thus began the independent and separate property of house-members*, with the first great blow which the old family system received at the hand of the Imperial Government. It is interesting to note that this is exactly what happened in the beginning of the Roman Empire, when *castrense pcclium* of filiusfamilias was recognized for military services, and three centuries afterward *quasi-castrense peclium* for civil services.

The issue of a law in 1872, which abolished the prohibition of the sale of land, and *granted title-deeds to landowners*, the issue, in the following year, of the *government bonds* for public loans, and the *establishment of joint stock companies and savings-banks* mark the next step in the development of the separate property of house-members. The courts of Law began to recognize house-members' separate property in the title-deeds, bonds, stocks, debentures or savings which they held in their own names, and thus *individual property began to grow up by the side of house-property*. But on the other hand, a Law (No. 275) was passed in 1872 to the effect, that the house-head should not be liable for the debts contracted by house-members, unless he became a surety to the contract.

Although the separate property of house-members was thus established, the rule of succession was not settled until the promulgation of the new Civil Code. As a rule, the property left by a deceased house-member went to the house-head. But here again, the Code took a decided step and gave the right of succession to the *nearest descendants equally, whether they were males or females, or whether they were in the same house with the deceased or not*, the right of representation being always given to the children of the pre-deceased descendant. After descendants comes the consort; next in order, the lineal ascendant; and *as the last successor, the house-head.* Other rules relating to this kind of succession do not differ much from those we find in Western countries.

By comparing the above mentioned two kinds of succession, we shall notice that they present a remarkable contrast and indicate the transient stage in which the Japanese law of succession finds itself. The rules relating to succession to house-headship rest chiefly upon indigenous elements, while those relating to succession to property are based principally upon Western ideas.

XVIII. Succession inter vivos.

Another characteristic of the Japanese succession law is the existence of Succession *inter vivos*, side by side with Succession *mortis causa.* The succession which arises during the lifetime of the person succeeded, takes place only with reference to *succession to house-headship;* for house-headship may come to an end either by *a house-head's death or the loss of house-headship during his life-time.* Succession *inter vivos* takes place in the following cases:—

I. "Inkyo" or abdication of house-headship.

II. Loss of nationality by a house-head.

III. The marriage of a famale house-head.

IV. The divorce of a husband who has married a female house-head.

V. When a house-head leaves the house in consequence of the invalidation of his marriage or adoption.

I will explain each of the causes of succession *inter vivos* in order.

i. "Inkyo" or abdication of house-headship.

House-headship is not a lifelong authority. It may be lost in several ways, the most usual of which is its abdication or "inkyo" which literally means "*living in retirement.*" The origin of this custom has been sometimes ascribed to Buddhism, but I have shown in a work especially devoted to this subject ("Inkyo-ron" or "Treatise on Abdication" 1891.) that this institution was originally derived from China, and developed among us by the influence of Buddhism and Feudalism. The abdication of house-headship may be classified with reference to its *causes* under the following *four heads;* namely, 1st, Religious Abdication, 2nd, Political Abdication, 3rd, Judicial Abdication and 4th, Physiological Abdication.

(1) Religious Abdication.

After the introduction of Buddhism the practice gradually grew up, among higher classes, of withdrawing from active life when any person attained "the age of retirement" which was *seventy* according to the Chinese Ritual Code, and closing his days in religious devotion as a hermit or priest. Our history abounds in instances where ministers of state tendered their resignations for the purpose of devoting the rest of their lives to religious practice. As I have already said, house-headship was rather an institution of public law than of private law, and the *resignation of office usually brought with it the loss of house-headship.* In later times, the middle and lower classes, began to imitate the example set by the heads of noble families, until it has become a general custom among the people. Until recently, it was a very common practice for retired persons to shave their heads, like Buddhist priests, in token of their having given up secular business and of having embraced the religious life. It was for this reason that the designation of "niudō-inkyo" or "priestly retirement" was employed for this kind of abdication.

This practice is very common among the Hindoo whose life is distributed into three periods, namely the Student, Householder and Ascetic periods. Minute regulations as to the life of the ascetic are contained in Hindoo law books, especially in the sixth chapter of the Code of Manu. Entering into a monastery seems to have had the same effect as death in the early Germanic and English laws (Young's Anglo-saxon Family Law, Co Litt. 133, Blaxland's Codex legum Anglicanarum p. 217.) and in the French law before the Revolution (Zachariae, Franz. Civilrecht § 162.), but since the abolition of civil death in modern legal systems succession *inter vivos* does not occur in European Families of Law.

(2.) Political Abdication.

From an early period of our history, it was very common for the upper and middle classes to resort to abdication for various political reasons. Sometimes it was made use of by unscrupulous minister of State or influential servants of Daimios to deprive masters of their power, and put other persons, perhaps puppets, in their places; sometimes, house-heads retired in order to shift responsibilities to other persons' shoulders, and wield real power themselves, or pull strings from behind the curtain; or sometimes they gave up the worldly life and led the ascetic life out of political discontent or disappointment.

(3) Legal Abdication.

I mean by *legal abdication* the compulsory loss of house-headship by way of punishment or atonement for a crime or other grave fault. Cases occurred very frequently during the Feudal times, especially under the Tokugawa Shogunate, in which a house-head was sentenced or ordered to abdicate as a punishment for his offence. Particular names have been given to this kind of abdication, such as "Zaikwa-inkyo" or "penal abdication"; or "Chikkyo-inkyo" or "confinement abdication"; or "Tsutsushimi-inkyo" or "reprimand-abdication." House-heads were also very often forced to abdicate by the resolution of family councils on account of their moral depravity, which made them unfit for the duties of house-headship. Even in the beginning of the present reign, this kind of abdication continued; and Art. 14 of the Criminal Code of 1873 provided that Kwazoku and Shizoku or nobles and samurais who were guilty of crimes, involving grave moral depravity, should be sentenced to the loss of house-headship, together with their privileges.

(4.) Physiological Abdication.

The decay of physical or mental power either on account of old age or ill health is the most common cause of abdication. Manu says "When a householder sees his skin wrinkled, and his hair white, and the sons of his sons, then he may resort to the forest" (Manu. VI. 2.). As house-headship was an institution of *public law as well as of private law*, it involved not only power over the house-members, but also many duties toward the state, besides duties and responsibilities toward the house-members, which were incumbent upon that position. So, house-heads were often obliged to retire from the active duties of family life, when their age or state of health made them unfit for that position. This was especially the case with the samurai class during the *Feudal period, when physical power was especially necessary for the discharge of military duties.* It is for this reason that abdication came to be regarded as an important and necessary institution, and *laws relating to it made great progress under the military régime of Feudalism.*

The rule with regard to the *age* at which a house-head was allowed to abdicate was *seventy* before the establishment of the Feudal System, which was the age of retirement according to the Chinese Ceremonial Code (禮記). But *this age was lowered under Feudalism* and *fifty* was fixed as the lowest limit of the age at which a house-head was allowed to abdicate without adducing any other reason. But since the abolition of Feudalism and the establishment of the conscription system, which imposes military duty irrespective of a man's position in the house, there is no need to keep this low limit of age. *The new Code raised it again and fixed it at sixty*; so that there have been *three changes* as to the age of retirement, the 1st being seventy, the 2nd fifty and the 3rd sixty.

According to the new Code, a house-head may abdicate when he has attained the age of sixty, but in case of a female house-head, she may abdicate irrespective of her age (Civil

Code. Art. 752 & 755.) In all other cases, the permission of a court of law is necessary. Such permission is given, if a house-head is unable to continue the management of the house owing to one of the following causes; namely, sickness, the necessity of succeeding as heir to the headship of the main branch of the family, or of resuscitating it, the desire to enter another house by marriage, or other unavoidable causes. (Civil Code. Art. 753 & 784.) In both these cases, there must always be an heir to succeed him in the headship of the house; for nobody but a person who has founded a new house may abolish it, as the abolition of a house would bring with it, in other cases, the extinction of the worship of the ancestors. (Civil Code. Art. 762 & 763.)

Loss of Nationality.

The house system is a *national institution*, and foreigners not being considered as belonging to any house, the house-headship necessarily comes to an end when a house-head loses his nationality, by naturalization or other causes mentioned in the Law of Nationality (Law No. 66. 1899); just as a Roman *paterfamilias* lost his *patria potestas* on account of the loss of citizenship by undergoing *media capitis diminutio*.

The Marriage of a Female House-head.

According to Art. 736 of the Civil Code, if a female house-head marries, the husband enters the house of his wife, instead of the wife's entering the husband's house according to the usual rule, and at once becomes the house-head, unless the parties concerned expressed a contrary intention at the time of marriage. Thus successsion *inter vivos* to the house-headship occurs in case of the marriage of a female house-head.

The Divorce of a Husband who has married a Female House-head.

As the husband entered the house and has become the house-head in consequence of the marriage, he leaves the house by divorce, and at the same time loses the house-headship. Thus divorce in this case becomes a cause of succession *inter vivos*.

v. Invalidation of Marriage or Adoption.

If a man who married a female house-head, or an adopted son or daughter has become a house-head, and the marriage or the adoption is invalidated for one of the causes mentioned in the Code, the husband or the adopted child leaves the house and the house-headship is lost. In this case, as the invalidation has no retrospective effect, the preceding house-head, though alive, such as the wife or the abdicated adoptive father, does not recover the house-headship as if there had been no marriage or adoption, but the rules of succession apply just as in the case of death.

The above enumeration of the causes will show that succession *inter vivos*, which is not usually found in modern laws, occurs very frequently under the present Japanese law.

XIX. Conclusion.

I hope I have been able to show, to some extent at least, that the new Japanese Civil Code furnishes valuable materials for students of historical and comparative jurisprudence. The Codification was the result of the great political and social revolutions which took place within a comparatively short period. The Code embodies in itself archaic and modern elements on the one hand, and Eastern and Western elements on the other. Within the past thirty years, Japanese law has passed from the Chinese Family of Law to the European Family; the notion of right was introduced; woman's position was raised from a condition of total subjection to one of equality with man, as far as private rights are concerned; the status of foreigners advanced from the stage of enmity to that of equality with citizens; the family system was greatly modified; the separate property of house-members began to be recognized; and property succession has come to exist side by side with the succession of house-headship.

Comparing the new Japanese Civil Code with Western Codes, we observe great similarity between them in the first three Books relating to General Provisions, Real Rights and Obligations respectively, but great difference in the last two, which relate to Family and Succession. Of the first three Books, the law of obligations may be said to be entirely Occidental. That part of law may indeed be said to be in a sense cosmopolitan, the laws of different countries exhibiting a relatively small amount of variation in this regard. The law of obligations, therefore, has the greatest propagating capacity and is generally first received in other countries. Next comes the law relating to movables. But land is usually so bound up with the public policy and local conditions of a country, that we usually find much divergence in the laws relating to immovables in different countries. The laws relating to Succession and Family, depending, as they do, upon the national character, religion, history, traditions and customs, show the least capacity for assimilation. So, the usnal order of assimilation, or reception of foreign laws is, (1) Law of Obligation (2) Law of Movables, (3) Law of Immovables, (4) Law of Succession and Family.

I have not touched upon those parts of the Civil Code, which relate to Obligations and Rights *in rem*, because the rules relating to these parts are mostly derived from Western jurisprudence and will present little that is novel to a European or American audience. I have confined my remarks, therefore, to thoss parts in which the indigenous element is usually most persistent. I have shown that even in these, we have made great reforms since the opening of the country to foreign intercourse. During the last thirty years we have been trying to adopt from Western civilization whatever seemed to us best fitted for the progress of the country.

We now possess a Civil Code based upon the most advanced principles of Western jurisprudence. But the Code is only a framework or skeleton of law. What supplies flesh, blood and sinews to it is the integrity and learning of the Bench and the Bar, and the law-abiding habit of the people. But, above all, the fountain-head of legal improvement is legal science. Law is national or territorial, but the science of law is universal, and is not confined within the bounds of any state. We have profited in the past by the work of scientific jurists of the West, and we must look, in future, to the mutual assistance and co-operation of the scientific brotherhood of the world.

学術選書プラス
5
民　法

The New Japanese Civil Code:
新日本民法典

2011(平成23)年６月30日　第１版第１刷発行
1255-6：P288　¥32000E-013：030-010-005

著　者　穂　積　陳　重
発行者　今井　貴　稲葉文子
発行所　株式会社　信　山　社
編集第２部
〒113-0033　東京都文京区本郷6-2-9-102
Tel 03-3818-1019　Fax 03-3818-0344
info@shinzansha.co.jp
東北支店　仙台市青葉区子平町11番１号208・112
笠間才木支店　〒309-1611　茨城県笠間市笠間515-3
Tel 0296-71-9081　Fax 0296-71-9082
笠間来栖支店　〒309-1625　茨城県笠間市来栖2345-1
Tel 0296-71-0215　Fax 0296-72-5410

出版契約　2011-1255-6-01011　Printed in Japan

 印刷・製本／ワイズ書籍・渋谷文泉閣
ISBN978-4-7972-1255-6　C3332　分類324-000：a005
1255-01011：013-030-010-005：P32000E
NDC 分類324.000-a005

新日本民法典講義（第2改訂版）

Lectures on the New Japanese Civil Code:
as material for the study of compatative jurisprudence,

by ***Nobushige Hozumi***

Second & Revised Edition

1912

新日本民法典講義（第２改訂版）

（東京帝国大学名誉教授・穂積陳重著）

[Includes index]

THE MARUZEN KABUSHIKI-KAISHA, TOKYO, OSAKA & KYOTO.

学術選書プラス
5
民　法

2011 復刊

SHINZANSHA

信 山 社

進呈

THE

NEW JAPANESE CIVIL CODE

AS MATERIAL FOR THE STUDY OF COMPARATIVE JURISPRUDENCE

THE ITALIAN TRANSLATION

BY SIGNORINA MARIA SCIALOJA

IL NUOVO CODICE CIVILE GIAPPONESE

QUALE MATERIALE PER LO STUDIO

DEL DIRITTO COMPARATO

SOCIETÀ EDITRICE LIBRARIA

MILANO

BY THE SAME AUTHOR

ANCESTOR-WORSHIP & JAPANESE LAW

SECOND EDITION

THE GERMAN TRANSLATION

OF THE FIRST EDITION

BY DR. PAUL BRUNN

DER EINFLUSS DES AHNENKULTUS

AUF DAS

JAPANISCHE RECHT

THE MARUZEN KABUSHIKI-KAISHA

TOKYO, OSAKA & KYOTO

LECTURES

ON THE

New Japanese Civil Code

AS MATERIAL FOR THE STUDY OF
COMPARATIVE JURISPRUDENCE

BY

NOBUSHIGE HOZUMI

HOGAKU-HAKUSHI

HONORARY PROFESSOR OF THE IMPERIAL UNIVERSITY OF TOKYO,
MEMBER OF THE IMPERIAL ACADEMY OF JAPAN,
BARRISTER-AT-LAW, OF THE MIDDLE TEMPLE, ENGLAND

Second & Revised Edition

THE MARUZEN KABUSHIKI-KAISHA
TOKYO, OSAKA & KYOTO

1912

PREFACE

Early in 1904, I received a communication from Dr. Simon Newcomb, President of the Congress of Arts and Science, that the Administrative Board of the Louisiana Purchase Exposition had chosen me as one of the foreign speakers on the subject of Comparative Law at the International Congress of Arts and Science, which was to be held in September in connection with the Exposition, and that he had been authorized to extend to me an invitation to attend the Congress and deliver an address on the above-named subject. The plan of the Congress was based on the happy and original idea of collecting and exhibiting at the Exposition, not only the material and visible products of scientific thoughts, but the scientific thoughts themselves, which had produced these results. For that purpose, the authorities of the Exposition had appropriated a large sum of money and had amply provided for the travelling expenses of the foreign speakers. The communication further intimated, that the original plan was to invite, aside from Americans, only European scholars, but that the Administrative Board had approved and adopted the recommendation of the Organizing Committee that Japanese scholars should also be included. Accordingly, invitations were extended to Baron D. Kikuchi, Dr. S. Kitazato and myself. My appreciation of the honor thus conferred upon me was sufficient to induce me to accept the invitation, inspite of not a little personal inconvenience. My address was given on the 24th of September. Of that address, more or less rewritten and much amplified, this small book is the outcome.

I take this opportunity of expressing my thanks to the officers of the Exposition and of the Congress, especially the Hon. David Francis, President of the Exposition, Dr. Howard J. Rogers, Director of the Congresses, the late Dr. Simon Newcomb, President of the Congress, Prof. Hugo Münsterberg and Prof. Albion W. Small, Vice-presidents of the Congress, Dr. R. H. Jesse, Dr. H. S. Pritchet, Dr. Herbert Putnam, Dr. N. M. Butler, Dr. William R. Harper and the Hon. Frederick J. V. Skiff, members of the Administrative Board, for the hospitality and courtesy which they showed us during our stay in St. Louis, and which made that stay one of the most pleasant and useful experiences of my life.

I must also express my great obligation to my late colleague Prof. Charles Sumner Griffin, who kindly read over the original manuscript of my lecture, and gave me many valuable suggestions as to corrections and improvements. But it gives me pain to reflect that the acknowledgement of my obligation on this page comes now too late. It might have given him pleasure—certainly it would have given me great satisfaction—could I have expressed my obligation to him personally—an obligation, alas, which it is now impossible to repay!

My thanks are also due to Mr. K. Hanazono and my son Shigetō Hozumi for reading the proof-sheets and otherwise assisting me in preparing this lecture for the second edition.

NOBUSHIGE HOZUMI.

Tokyo, July, 1912.

CONTENTS

PREFACE

I

INTRODUCTION 1
Japanese Law and comparative jurisprudence . 2

II

CAUSES OF THE CODIFICATION 3
(1) The great social and political changes . . 3
Commodore Perry's visit 3
" Expulsion of foreigners and loyalty to the Emperor " 4
The opening of the country 5
The Restoration of 1868 5
The Five Articles of the Imperial Oath . 6
The abolition of the Feudal System . 7
(2) The abolition of extraterritorial jurisdiction. 10
Bureau for the Investigation of Institutions (1870) 12
Committee for the Compilation of the Civil Code (1875) 13
The draft of 1878 13
Bureau for the Codification of the Civil Law (1881) 13
Boissonade's draft 13
Committee for the Investigation of Law (1886) 13
The Civil Code of 1890 14
The " Postponement Campaign " . . 15
State of legal education in Japan . . 16
The Codification Committee 19
The Drafting sub-committee 20
The new Civil Code of 1896 and 1898 . 23

III

Objects of the Codification 25
Social revolution and codification 25
Four objects of codification 25
(1) Pacification 25
(2) Innovation 26
(3) Unification 26
(4) Simplification 27
Three great epochs in Japanese history . . 27
The Taihō Code of 702 27
The Jōyei Shikimoku of 1232 28
The Civil Code of 1896 and 1898 28

IV

Methods of Comparative Jurisprudence . . . 29
Three methods of comparison 29
Indigenous and foreign elements in the law . 31
Kinship between laws of two countries . . 32
Mother-law and Filial-law 32
Genealogical method 33

V

Great Families of Law 35
Seven Great Families 35
(1) The Family of Chinese law 35
(2) The Family of Hindu law 35
(3) The Family of Mohamedan law . . . 35
(4) The Family of Roman law 35
(5) The Family of Germanic law 35
(6) The Family of Slavonic law 35
(7) The Family of English law 35

VI

The Position of the Japanese Civil Code among Legal Systems of the World 36

Introduction of Chinese civilization and the Taihō-Codes 36
The Criminal Code of 1870 37
Introduction of Western civilization and the new Codes 37
The Revised Criminal Code of 1873 . . . 37
The "principles of reason and justice" . . . 38
Influence of the Law Schools, the Bench and the Bar 39
The new Codes 40

VII

THE PUBLICATION OF THE CODE 42
Change in the conception of law 42
Publication was not essential 42
Secrecy of the law 42
Laws were commands to officials 44
Three stages in the idea of law 45
(1) People as passive object of the operation of the law 46
(2) People as party to the operation of the law 47
(3) People as party to the making of the law 47

VIII

THE ARRANGEMENT OF THE CODE 49
Boissonade's system 49
Pandekten-System 50
Arrangement of the new Code 50
General Provisions 50
The Family Law 51
The Succession Law 51
Family-unit and individual-unit 52
Three stages in the evolution of succession law . 54

Status-succession and property-succession . . . 55

IX

The Introduction of the Notion of Right . 56
Law and right 56
Notion of duty 56
"Bun" 57
"Ken-ri" 57
Law as rules of duty 58
Law as rules of right 58

X

The Legal Position of Woman 60
Three periods in the legal position of woman . 60
The first period 60
Primitive simplicity and absence of artificial doctrines 61
The second period 61
Influence of Chinese moral philosophy . . 62
The doctrine of "three obediences" . . 62
Buddhism and Feudalism 63
The third period 64
Influence of European civilization . . . 64
Female education 64
The new Civil Code 64
Laws relating to married woman's property . 67
Four systems 67
(1) System of Conjugal Unity 67
(2) System of Dowry 68
(3) System of Community 68
(4) System of Separate Property . . . 68
The new Civil Code 69
Law of divorce 70
Seven grounds of divorce 70

Abandonment and divorce 71
Two kinds of divorce 72
(1) Consensual divorce 72
(2) Judicial divorce 73

XI

THE STATUS OF FOREIGNERS 75
Four principles of the law 75
(1) Enmity 75
(2) Inferiority 75
(3) Reciprocity 76
(4) Equality 77
Three periods in the legal position of foreigners. 77
(1) Period of Exclusion 78
(2) Period of Treaty Rights 78
(3) Period of Legal Rights 79
Foreign juridical persons 79
Equal enjoyment of private rights 80
Foreigner's right to own land 81

XII

THE HOUSE AND KINSHIP 85
Double bases of the family law 85
House-head and house-members 85
Constitution of a house 86
Kinship 87
Maine on the ancient family 89
The Japanese house and the Roman family . 91

XIII

THE HOUSE-HEADSHIP AND THE PARENTAL POWER. 95
Parental power limited by the conception of the house 96
House-headship and patria potestas . . . 97
Natural relationship and artificial connection . 98

CONTENTS

XIV

RELATIONSHIP 100
Consanguinity and family rank 101
Kindred of the Five Ranks 101
" Superior kins " and " inferior kins " . . . 104
The Chinese law of mourning 104
Five classes of mourning dresses 105
The " Bukki-Ryō " or the Mourning Law . . 107

XV

LAW OF PERSONAL REGISTRATION AND THE CIVIL CODE 108
Three stages in the law of personal registration 109
(1) Epoch of Clan-registration 109
(2) Epoch of House-registration 109
(3) Epoch of Status-registration 109
Clan-headship 109
" Great Clans " and " Small Clans " 110
Clans as administrative divisions 110
Register of Clan-names 112
House-register 112
Law of House-registration 113
The Clan and the Family 114

XVI

ADOPTION 115
Maine on adoption 115
Adoption classified with regard to its object . 117
(1) Succession to Family Worship 117
(2) Succession to House-headship 117
(3) Succession to Property 117
(4) Charity or Consolation 117
Ancestor-worship and adoption 117
Childlessness 117

Adopter's age 118
Kinship 119
"Muko-yōshi" or "adoption of son-in-law" . 120
Feudalism and adoption 121
"Geidō-yōshi" or "arts-adoption" . . . 122
"Kiu-yōshi" or "quick adoption" . . . 123
Adoption by a house-member 125
Will and adoption 125

XVII

SUCCESSION IN GENERAL—THE EVOLUTION IN THE LAW OF SUCCESSION 127
Three stages 127
(1) Succession to worship 127
(2) Succession to status 127
(3) Succession to property 127
The Taihō Code 128
"Katoku" 129
Four kinds of heirs 131
(1) Legal heir 131
Causes of disinheritance 133
(2) Appointed heir 134
(3) Chosen heir 134
Order of choosing an heir 134
"House-daughter" 134
(4) Ascendant heir 135

XVIII

PROPERTY SUCCESSION—THE RECOGNITION OF HOUSE-MEMBER'S SEPARATE PROPERTY 137
House-member's right before the Restoration . 138
House-member's right after the Restoration . 138
House-property and individual property . . 139
Order of inheritance 140

XIX

Succession *inter vivos* 142
Five causes of succession *inter vivos* . . . 142
i. Abdication of house-headship . . . 143
(1) Religious abdication 144
" Nyūdō-inkyo " 145
(2) Political abdication 146
(3) Legal abdication 146
" Zaikwa-inkyo " 147
" Chikkyo-inkyo " 147
" Tsutsushimi-inkyo " 147
(4) Physiological abdication . . . 148
Age of abdication 149
ii. Loss of nationality 151
iii. Marriage of a female house-head . . 151
iv. Divorce of a female house-head . . . 152
v. Invalidation of marriage or adoption . 152

XX

Conclusion 154

The New Japanese Civil Code, as Material for the Study of Comparative Jurisprudence

I

INTRODUCTION

In responding to the call of the Committee of the Congress to deliver a lecture on Comparative Law, I have, for reasons which will not be far to seek, taken the new Japanese Civil Code as the subject of my discourse. If, at the outset, I may be allowed to use a paradoxical expression in characterizing that law-book, I should say that "the East and the West, the Past and the Present meet in the new Japanese Civil Code." I mean that the codification of private law in Japan was the result of the great political and social revolution, which followed the opening of the country and the introduction of Western ideas; so that the Code embodies in itself both archaic and modern elements on the one hand, and Oriental and Occidental elements on the other. It is, so to speak, a connecting link between the Past and the Present, between the East and the West, and stands at the cross-roads of historical and comparative jurisprudence. It is, on that account, peculiarly interesting to scientific jurists, as supplying them with materials which few other systems can furnish. It will be my endeavour, in this lecture, to show the effect which the contact of the Western civilization with that of the East has produced on the civil law of the country, thereby illustrating some of the leading principles of the evolution of law by reference to the rules of the Code. The scope of my lecture being so wide, and the time for its delivery being limited, I shall confine myself to those characteristic features of the Code, which are not usually found in Occidental jurisprudence.

II

Causes of the Codification

In order to set forth the characteristics of the Japanese Civil Code, it will be useful, first of all, briefly to explain the causes which led to the codification, and give a short sketch of the history of its compilation. The principal causes of the reform and codification of the civil law are following.

The first is to be found in the great *social and political changes*, which have taken place since the opening of the country to foreign intercourse, especially since the Restoration of the Emperor to actual power in 1868. It was just half a century ago, that Commodore Perry knocked at our doors to open the country to foreign intercourse. Aroused from the deep slumber of centuries, we rubbed our eyes, and saw Western civilization confronting us, but it was some time before we were wide awake, and realized the advantage of introducing it into our country.

In a country which had remained entirely secluded for centuries from the rest of the world, it was quite natural, that distrust, which in many cases grew to be hatred, of foreigners should, at first, have existed among the mass of the people; and that the cry of "jō-i" or "the expulsion of foreigners" should have been raised among them. Many far-sighted statesmen and scholars, however, clearly saw the necessity of introducing Western civilization and of adopting whatever seemed conducive to the intellectual or material progress of the country, in order that Japan might become a member of the family of nations. There were others, who, while understanding very well the necessity of introducing Western civilization, joined the anti-foreign party, in order to hasten the overthrow of the Shogunate Government, for, although the expression "Sonnō-jōi," or "Loyalty to the Emperor, and the expulsion of foreigners," which was in vogue at that time, among enthusiastic patriots, contained two things which had no necessary connection with each other, it was adopted as watchword by the party of political reform, in order to set the mass of the people against the Shogun's government. But, as soon as their object was attained, and the present Emperor was restored to real power, they threw off the mask and kept only the former half of their watchword "Sonnō," or "Loyalty to the Emperor."

The first act of the Emperor, on ascending the throne, was to enunciate the fundamental principles of his government in the form of a solemn oath, which has since been known as the "Imperial Oath of the Five Articles." The Five Articles and the term of the oath are as follows :—

(1) Deliberative assemblies shall be established and all measures of government shall be decided by public opinion.

(2) All classes, high and low, shall unite in vigorously carrying out the plan of the government.

(3) Officials, civil and military, and all common people shall, as far as possible, be allowed to fulfill their just desires, so that there may not be any discontent among them.

(4) Uncivilized customs of former times shall be broken through, and everything shall be based upon just and equitable principles of nature.

(5) *Knowledge shall be sought for throughout the world*, so that the welfare of the Empire may be promoted.

"Desiring to carry out a reform without parallel in the annals of Our country, We Ourselves here take the initiative and swear to the Deities of Heaven and Earth to adopt these fundamental principles of national government, so as to establish thereby the security and prosperity of the people. We call upon you all to make combined and strenuous effort to carry them out."[1]

This oath has been made the basis of our national policy. How well the Emperor has kept his oath, and how unswervingly his government and his people have followed the wish expressed by their sovereign, is shown by the subsequent events of our history.

The Feudal System was abolished, and all the *Daimios* or feudal lords voluntarily surrendered their fiefs to the Emperor, together with their powers to make laws, issue paper-currency and exercise both civil and criminal jurisdiction within their dominions. The four hereditary classes of the people, namely the *Samurai* or soldiers, farmer, artisans and merchants were abolished, and all could freely choose their own profession or calling. Officials were no longer appointed on account of birth,

---

[1] I have followed the translation of the epilogue to the oath by Baron D. KIKUCHI as the most faithful. See his *Japanese Education*, p. 45.

as was formerly the case, but on account of personal merits, and even the lowest born could aspire to become the highest official of the State. The family system was, as I shall show presently, gradually weakened, so that the individual began to take the place of the family as the unit of society. Schools for both sexes have been established in all parts of the Empire, which are open to all classes without the least distinction. Higher education is no longer the monopoly of the *Samurai* and the clergy. Students and officials have been yearly sent to Europe and America, to study different branches of art and science, or to investigate and report upon the methods and resources of Western civilization. Christianity which had been very strictly forbidden during the Tokugawa Shogunate, was gradually tolerated under the new government of the Emperor, until at last freedom of religious belief and worship was secured by Art. 28 of the Constitution promulgated in 1889. The introduction of steamships, railroads, electric telegraphs etc. completely changed the means of communication and travelling both on land and sea. The opening of the country to foreign trade, and the changes in commerce and industry at home by the establishment of banking and other commercial firms and factories in different parts of the country, brought about great economical revolutions among the people. The Imperial Household abolished the old ceremonial costumes, and adopted European dress for ceremonial occasions both for men and women. The *Samurai* threw off the two swords which they had regarded as their *souls;* the men cut off their queue and had their hair dressed in Western fashion; they discarded their loose native dress and began to wear tight practical European dress; they now build their government offices, schools and other public buildings after the European style; they began to eat beef, the partaking of which had been regarded as something sacrilegious. It is needless to say that these political, economical and social revolutions, which extended to every department of life, occasioned the necessity for corresponding reforms in the laws of the country, which could not be met by fragmentary legislations. Sweeping legislation by way of codification was the only way of keeping up with the rapid strides, which Japan had taken during the past four decades.

The second and more immediate cause of the codification of the civil law was the earnest desire on the part of the Japanese people to put an end to the existence of the *extra-territorial jurisdiction* which had been granted by earlier treaties to the sixteen Treaty Powers of Europe and America, and to resume the civil and criminal jurisdiction over the subjects and citizens of the Treaty Powers, residing or travelling in the country. At the time, when we first entered into commercial treaties with Western Powers, it was quite natural and reasonable, that they should demand the reservation to themselves of jurisdiction over their own respective subjects and citizens. This was indeed necessitated by the great difference between their own laws and institutions and those of Japan, while the habits and customs of the people were also quite unlike. We saw the necessity and justice of acceding to their demand, but, at the same time, felt that the existence of such a legal anomaly was a disgrace to the country, and wholly incompatible with that scrupulous regard for the integrity of territorial sovereignty, which ought to characterize the intercourse of independent friendly nations. So, from an early date in the present reign, attempts were repeatedly made to revise the treaties and expunge from them the abominable extra-territorial clause. But, every time, we were met by the objection that our laws were incomplete. Although as a matter of principle, we did not admit the justice of the foreigners' objection to obeying the laws of the country to which they chose to resort, we were obliged, in fairness, to recognize the reasonableness of their objections.

After many years of difficult diplomatic negotiations, it was at last agreed, that the treaties should be revised and the extra-territoriality should be abolished; and, at the same time, the Japanese government undertook to frame codes of laws and put them in operation before the new treaties should go into effect.

The above-mentioned two causes, one internal and the other external, combined to make the work of codification one of the most urgent necessities of the time. As a preliminary step to the work of codification, a Bureau for the Investigation of Institutions was established in the third year of Meiji (1870) and one of the fruits of the labour of that Bureau was the translation of the French Codes. This translation afforded the knowledge-thirsty Japanese ideas of Western laws for the first time, and had an immense influence upon subsequent legislation and judicial decisions in the courts of law. In 1875, a Committee for the Compilation of the Civil Code was appointed for the first time. In 1878, a draft was submitted by this Committee to the Government. This draft was a close imitation of the French Civil Code, both in its arrangements and in its contents, and was not adopted by the Government. In 1880, Prof. Boissonade, an eminent French jurist, who was then a legal adviser to the Japanese Government, was asked to prepare a new draft, and in the next year, a Bureau for the Codification of the Civil Law was established, to which Prof. Boissonade's draft was submitted for deliberation. The Bureau was abolished in 1886, and a Committee for the investigation of Law was appointed, composed of the members of the *Genrō-in* or the Senate and of the Bench, with Count Yamada, the Minister of Justice, at its head. This committee made its report in 1888, and the draft was submitted to the deliberation of the Senate and was adopted by that Council. On the 27th of March, 1890, under Law No. 28, those parts of the Code which were drafted by Prof. Boissonade, that is, Book II, relating to "Property in General," Book III, relating to the "Means of Acquiring Property," Book IV, "Security of Rights *in personam*" and Book V, relating to "Evidence" were published. Those parts which were prepared by Japanese jurists, namely, Book I, relating to "Persons" and part of Book III, relating to "Succession" were published on the 16th of October of the same year; and the whole Code was to go into operation from the 1st of January 1893.

Thus after the arduous toil of fifteen years, Japan possessed a code of private law for the first time in her history. It was quite natural that the Code should become a topic of earnest consideration for all educated classes of the people. Especially among lawyers and politicians, a violent controversy arose regarding the merits of the new Code. Those jurists, who had studied English law in the Tokio Imperial University or in England or America, first raised their voices against the Code and demanded the postponement of the date of its going into operation, with a view to its complete revision. The French section of Japanese lawyers, on the other hand, supported the Code and insisted upon the necessity of its going into operation at the date originally appointed. The German section of jurists, whose number was at that time comparatively small, was divided into two parties, some siding with the one, others joining the other. Japanese lawyers were thus divided into two hostile camps, and the lively discussion which arose among them, is known as the "Postponement Campaign." The arguments pro and con put forward for the postponement and revision of the Code were many and were of varying importance. To outsiders, the campaign may have seemed like a sectarian conflict between the English and French groups of Japanese lawyers. But this struggle is eminently interesting to scientific observers of the general history of law, for it was, in reality, a contest of the Historical School with the School of Natural Law, resembling in many respects the famous controversy between Savigny and Thibaut in the beginning of the same century. This question contained an important issue, as to which theory should have a predominant influence over the jurisprudence and legislation of the country.

In order to explain this interesting event in our legal history, I must, for a moment, stop to give an account of the state of legal education in Japan at that time. English law had been taught in the Imperial University of Tokio since 1874 by English, American and Japanese teachers, and also in other law schools, and a great number of the graduates had, by that time, already filled important positions on the Bench and at the Bar as well as in other places, both in and out of the Government. They were all taught the doctrines of Bentham, Austin and Maine, and most of them belonged to the school of positive law. On the other hand, there was a law school attached to the Department of Justice, in which French Law was taught by Prof. Boissonade and other French and Japanese teachers. There were also two or three other law schools in which French law was taught. The graduates of these schools, who also filled important positions, had been taught the doctrines of Natural Law. It was quite natural that the doctrines which lawyers had imbibed in their early days of studentship should have strongly influenced their views as to legislations in their maturer days. And thus arose two opposite schools among the lawyers of Japan. In 1887, just three years before the publication of the Civil Code, the Imperial University made a reform in the program of the College of Law. The French Law School of the

Department of Justice was transferred to the University, and at the same time, a German Law Section was newly established, so that there came to be three sections in the College of Law, besides a fourth which is devoted to Political Science. This tripartite division in the University law education could not fail to produce an enduring effect on the subsequent legislation of the country. The Civil Code had become law, before the Constitution came into force in 1890, and the question of the postponement of its operation had to be decided in the Imperial Diet. Accordingly, a bill was introduced at the session of 1892 in the House of Representatives to postpone the operation of the Code with a view to its revision. After several warm debates, the bill was passed by both Houses of the Imperial Diet and the operation of the Code was postponed by Law No. 8 until the 31st of December 1896. Thus, the so-called "Postponement Campaign" resulted in the victory of the

"Postponement Party;" and in the following year, a Codification Committee was established by an Imperial Edict. The constitution of this Committee affords a very important clue for understanding the character of the new Code. The committee, with Prince (then Marquis) Itō, then the prime minister, as its president, consisted of members of both Houses of the Diet, professors of the Imperial University, members of the Bench and the Bar, with other eminent jurists and leading representatives of commerce and industry. The number of the members varied from time to time, but throughout, care had been taken in the appointment of members to represent every interest in society and also to represent English, French and German Schools of Japanese lawyers. The "Postponement Campaign" was very fierce while it lasted, but when the question was once settled, both parties threw off their animosity and joined hands in the work of giving the nation a code which would meet the exigencies of the time. The appointment of the three special members to prepare the draft also shows a conciliatory spirit on all sides. Professors Tomii, Umé and I were appointed to prepare the original draft which was to be submitted to the deliberation of the Committee. Professor Tomii, although he had studied law in Lyon and is *docteur en droit*, and thus belonged to the French School, sided with the "Postponement Party," and not only formed a remarkable exception among his comrades, but was one of the staunch advocate of postponement and revision. Professor Umé, who had studied law also in Lyon and is *docteur en droit*, was one of the champions of the "Anti-Postponement Party." I studied English law in the Inns of Court in London and am a member of the English Bar; and I belonged to the "Postponement Party." Both Prof. Umé and I also studied law in the University of Berlin, after we had finished our courses in France and England respectively. Thus, it will be seen that two out of the three framers of the Code represented the French Section, but one of them belonged to the "Postponement Party." While two belonged to the French and one to the English School, two of them had studied German law.

The constitution of the Committee, especially that of the Drafting Committee made it clear, that they could not agree to take the law of any one country as an exclusive model upon which to frame the new Code. Prof. Boissonade's draft was principally based upon the French Civil Code, but the framers of the revised Code agreed to collect the codes, statutes, and judicial reports of all civilized countries which existed in the English, French, German or Italian languages, besides international treaties which have reference to the rules of private law. They accordingly collected more than thirty civil codes, including many drafts, such as the draft of the Civil Code of New York, the draft of the German Code, the draft of the Belgian Code, besides other codes, statutes, reports and treaties, and comparing the rules or principles which existed in different countries, adopted whatever seemed to be best suited to the requirements of the country. In the original draft which was submitted to the deliberation of the Committee, an explanation was attached to each article, stating the reasons for the adoption of the rule. The corresponding articles or rules which existed in other countries as well as rules, precedents and customs in our own country were also cited for the consideration of the Committee. This method of preparing the draft gave a characteristic feature to the new Code. The Japanese Civil Code may be said to be a *fruit of comparative jurisprudence.* At first sight, it may appear that the new Code was very closely modeled upon the new German Civil Code; and I have very often read statements to that effect. It is true that the first and second draft of the German Code furnished very valuable material to the drafting committee and had a great influence upon the deliberations of the Committee. But, on close examination of the principles and rules adopted in the Code, it will appear that they gathered materials from all parts of the civilized world, and freely adopted rules or principles from the laws of any country, whenever they saw the advantage of doing so. In some parts, rules were adopted from the French Civil Code; in others, the principles of English common law were followed; in others again, such laws as the Swiss Federal Code of Obligations of 1881, the new Spanish Civil Code of 1889, the Property Code of Montenegro, Indian Succession and Contract Acts or the Civil Codes of Louisiana, Lower Canada or the South American Republics or the draft Civil Code of New York and the like have given materials for the framers of the Code. In January 1896, the report of the Committee on Book I, "General Provisions," Book II, "Rights *in rem*" and Book III, "Rights *in personam*" was submitted to the Imperial Diet and was adopted with only a few unimportant modifications. In April of the same year, these three Books were promulgated as Law No. 89. The remaining two Books on "Family" and "Succession" were submitted to the Imperial Diet in May 1898 and adopted by both Houses with only slight modifications, and were promulgated as Law No. 9 in June; and the whole Codes came into force on the 16th of July 1898.

The foregoing sketch, brief as it is, of the history of the codificatian of the civil law will be sufficient to show that the new Japanese Civil Code is the outcome of the comparative study of laws, and offers, in its turn, valuable materials for the study of comparative jurisprudence.

III

Objects of the Codification

I think it may be laid down as a general rule regarding the evolution of law, that *a comprehensive legislation generally follows a great social revolution.* If laws are social phenomena, it is quite natural that social changes should always bring with them corresponding changes in the laws of the country. The legal history of all nations, either ancient or modern, shows that the objects sought to be obtained by codification fall under one of the following four heads; namely, Pacification, Innovation, Unification and Simplification.

(1) Sometimes, codification takes place after a great social disturbance in order *to restore peace and maintain order by means of comprehensive legislation.* This was true of the ancient codes of Draco and Solon in Greece, the Law of the Twelve Tables in Rome, and the codifications

in China since the Han Dynasty, where it was customary for the founder of every dynasty to publish a new code of laws after he had gained the imperial power by force of arms. In Japan, the Codes of the Hōjō and the Tokugawa belong to this class.

(2) Laws are often codified either *to bring about a social reform*, or *to adjust the law to the requirements of the new state of things*, which has been brought about by social reform. To this class belong most of the codes, which have been promulgated in Japan since the Restoration of 1868.

(3) Very often codification takes place with a view to *the unification of different local laws and customs*, so that the country may be governed by a uniform code of laws. One of the objects of the Code Napoleon, the Italian Civil Code of 1865, and the new German

Imperial Codes was, in each case, the unification of the laws of the country. It was the principal object of the first Japanese Criminal Code of 1870, which was published soon after the Restoration, to establish unity in criminal law throughout the Empire by abolishing the particular laws which existed within the jurisdictions of the *Daimios*.

(4) Simplification of law by means of *logical arrangement* or *consolidation* of legal rules constitutes the most usual motive for codification in modern states.

Now, the majority of codifications, except sometimes those coming under the fourth class just mentioned, take place after great political or social revolutions, in consequence of which, pacification, innovation, unification or simplification becomes necessary. The history of codification in Japan amply exemplifies the above statement. The promulgation of the Taihō Code of 702 A.D. was the result of the great political and social revolution, which followed the introduction of Chinese civilization into the country. The next great codification, the framing of the Jōyei Shikimoku in 1232 A.D. under the Hojō Regency, was necessitated by the great political and social changes, which had taken place since the establishment of the Feudal System under the military government of the Shōguns. The new Japanese Civil Code is, as I have explained above, a result of the revolution which followed the opening of the country to foreign intercourse. Thus, *each of the three great epochs in Japanese history, the introduction of Chinese civilization, the establishment of Feudalism and the introduction of Western civilization, has been followed by codification.* The chief object of the Taihō Code, belonging to the first period, was Innovation; that of the Jōyei Shikimoku, belonging to the second period, was Pacification; while the framing of the new Civil Code had for its objects Innovation and Unification as well as Simplification.

IV

Methods of Comparative Jurisprudence

Looked at from another point of view, the new Japanese Civil Code may be taken as an illustration of the effect which the contact of Western with Eastern civilization has produced on the laws and institutions of the country. In this respect, I must first say a few words as to the methods of Comparative Jurisprudence. Hitherto, there have been three methods of comparison in vogue. One of them takes the *law of a particular state* as the unit of comparison, and comparing it with the laws of different states, finds similarities and divergencies among them, and deduces from them certain principles of law. This is the method generally adopted by jurists. In France, for instance, where comparative law is studied with greatest zeal, valuable materials for this method of investigation are furnished by the publications of the laws of different countries in the "Bulletin" and the "Annuaire" of the "Société de législation comparée" and by the numerous translations of foreign codes by Foucher, Antoine St. Joseph, Lehr, Dareste, Grasserie, Levé, Turrel, Prudhomme, Lepelletier and other eminent jurists.

There are others, who, perceiving that there are common features in the laws of each *race*, take a wider basis for their investigation and make the laws of particular races the units of comparison, and compare the one with the other.

There are others again, who take a still wider basis, and compare legal phenomena of different peoples without regard to nationality or race.

Of these three methods, the first may compare, for instance, English law with French, the second Germanic laws with Slavonic laws, while the third takes up, perhaps, the marriage laws and customs of European nations, American Indians, African negroes, Australians and Chinese.

All these three methods of comparison, which I have mentioned above, are useful for investigating the principles of law; and none of them can be rejected to the exclusive adoption of the other. But I think another method can be added to the list, which, though not hitherto employed, may be very advantageously adopted in the investigations of general principles of law. I mean a method which takes for the unit of comparison a certain group of laws having a *common lineage* or *descent.* If we examine the laws of different countries which have made a certain progress in civilization, we shall find that the law of each country consists of *two elements*; namely, the *indigenous element* and the *foreign element*; and except in uncivilized or barbarous communities which have no intellectual intercourse with other countries, instances are very rare, in which the law of any country is found consisting exclusively of indigenous elements. With the progress of means of communication and the consequent increase of intercourse among different peoples, the exchange, not only of material, but also of intellectual products becomes greater; and in regard to law, it may be laid down as a general rule that the *higher the community stands in the scale of civilization, the greater is the proportion of the foreign to the indigenous element.* This comes from what is called the reception or adoption of foreign laws.

Now, when the rules or principles of law of one country are adopted in another, there arises a sort of *kinship* between the laws of those two countries. One is descended from the other, and the *relationship, as it were, of ancestor and descendant is created between them.* The old law which served as a model or source of the new law may be called the "Parental Law" or "Mother-law" in relation to the new, which stands in a filial relation to the parental law.

The law of one country may be adopted in other countries *directly*, as Roman law was received in Germany, or *indirectly*, that is, it may be first adopted in one country, and then through that country, it may be received in the third, as European law, which has first been received in Japan, is now being introduced through her in China and Corea. Or again, the law of a mother country may be extended to her colonies or dependencies, as in the case with English law in British colonies.

In this way, the laws of all civilized countries may be divided into several groups, each comprising laws of many countries, but having common features and characteristics owing to their common origin. These different groups may be compared one with another, in order to find out uniformities and divergencies among them, and thus establish general principles of law. This method of comparative study of law, which may be called the *Genealogical Method*, to distinguish it from the other three, has the advantage, among many others, of combining the historical with the comparative method.

V

Great Families of Law

If, in order to take the Genealogical Method of comparison, we classify the laws existing at present in different parts of the world, we shall find that there are at least seven Great Families of Laws ; namely, (1) the Family of Chinese Law, (2) the Family of Hindu Law, (3) the Family of Mohamedan Law, (4) the Family of Roman Law, (5) the Family of Germanic Law (6) the Family of Slavonic Law, and (7) the Family of English Law. I have called these groups "the *Great Families of Laws*," because this classification is not meant to be exhaustive or exclusive. There are many smaller branches of law, not belonging to any of the above mentioned Families, which are, none the less, very important for the Genealogical Method of comparative study ; but for the purpose of the present lecture, they need not be mentioned here.

VI

The Position of the Japanese Civil Code among Legal Systems of the World

I have been at some length in explaining this method of comparative jurisprudence, in order to show the position of the new Japanese Civil Code in the general legal history of the world. Since the first introduction of Chinese civilization into our country, and the consequent Reform of the Taikwa Era (646 A.D.), the work of which was completed by the publication of the famous Taihō Codes in 701 A.D., *Japanese law has belonged to the Family of Chinese Law* for more than one thousand six hundred years; and notwithstanding many great changes in the laws and institutions of the country, which have taken place, since that time, the basis of Japanese laws and institutions has always been Chinese moral philosophy, together with the custom of Ancestor-worship and the Feudal system.

The Criminal Code (*Shin-ritsu-kōryō*) which was published in 1870, three years after the Restoration of 1868, was modeled upon the Chinese Codes of Tang, Min, and Shin Dynasty with certain modifications suggested by old Japanese laws. Only three years later, that code was revised, and a new code was published under the title of the Revised Criminal Code (*Kaitei-Ritsurei*). In the framing of that new Code, some European codes, especially the French, were consulted and adopted to a certain extent. Now, these two codes mark the transition period in the history of Japanese law. *The former was the last in the Chinese, and the latter the first in the European, system of legislation.* The Japanese law was at that time rapidly passing *from the Family of Chinese law to the Family of European laws.*

From the beginning of the present reign, the Imperial government was very active in making laws to meet the exigencies of the new state of things. But finding that such fragmentary legislation could not keep pace with the rapid progress of the nation and meet the requirements of the changing circumstances, the *Dajōgwan*, or the Great Council of State, which was then the supreme legislature, issued a Law (No. 103 in the 8th year of Meiji, 1875), which provided in Art. 3, that judges should decide civil cases according to the express provisions of written law, and in cases where there was no such written law, according to custom. In the absence of both written and customary laws, they were to decide *according to the principles of reason and justice.* This law flung wide open the door for the ingress of foreign law, and marks an epoch in Japanese legal history. Now, by this time, translations of the French Codes and other law books had appeared, and there were some judges on the Bench, though comparatively few at that time, who had studied English or French law. The rapidly changing circumstances of Japanese society brought many cases before the court, for which there were no express rules, written or customary, and the judges naturally sought to find out "the principles of reason and justice" in Western jurisprudence. The older members of the Bench, who had not been systematically taught in Western jurisprudence, consulted the translations of the French and other European Codes and text books, while the younger judges who had received systematic legal education in the Universities, either at home or abroad, and whose number increased from year to year, consulted Western Codes, statute books, law reports, and juridical treatises, and freely applied the principles of Occidental jurisprudence, which in their opinion, were conformable to reason and justice. Blackstone, Kent, Pollock, Anson, Langdel, Windscheid, Dernburg, Mourlon, Baudry-Lacantinerie and other text books and the numerous commentaries on European Codes, statute books and law reports were looked upon as repositories of the "principles of reason and justice" and supplied necessary data for their judgments. In this manner, Occidental jurisprudence entered our country, not only indirectly through the *University* and other law colleges, but also directly through the *Bench* and the *Bar*.

The above law, bold as it was, was only meant to be a temporary measure to supply the immediate wants of the changing society, until a complete and systematic code should have been compiled. In the meantime, the work of codification had been steadily proceeding, and resulted in the promulgation of the Criminal Code and the Code of Criminal Procedure in 1880, the Revised Code of Criminal Procedure, and the Code of Civil Procedure in 1890, the new Civil Code in 1896 and 1898, and Commercial Code in 1899.

What I have said above will suffice to show that the new Japanese Civil Code stands in a filial relation to the European systems, and *with the introduction of Western civilization, the Japanese civil law passed from the Chinese Family to the European Family of law.*

VII

The Publication of the Code

One of the most remarkable changes which the introduction of Western jurisprudence produced in Japan was the change in the *conception of law*. Previous to the Restoration of 1868, *there was no idea that publication was essential to law.* On the contrary, during the time of the Tokugawa Shogunate, most laws, especially the criminal code, were *kept in strict secrecy*. They were all in manuscript and were neither allowed to be printed nor published; and none but the judges and officials who were charged with the duty of carrying the rules into effect were allowed the perusal of the codes and the records of judicial precedents.

The famous Criminal Code of the Tokugawa Shogunate, commonly known as the "Hyakka-jō" or "The Hundred Articles" bears the following injunction at the end:—

"The above rules have been settled with His Highness' gracious sanction, and nobody except the magistrates shall be allowed to peruse them."

The subsequent compilation, called "Kwajō-rui-ten" contains the same injunction with the following addition:—

"Moreover, it is forever forbidden to make extracts from this Code, even of one article thereof." In 1841, thirteen authentic manuscript copies of the Code were made, and all the other copies and extracts which the clerks had made for their own use were ordered to be produced and burnt. One Ono Gonnojō and his son were severely punished for publishing a book which contained "The Hundred Articles" of the Code. An owner of a certain circulating library who had a manuscript book, showing the days on which the magistrates transacted business, or the "*dies fasti*" and "*nefasti*" of the judical court, was punished with banishment from his place of abode. These and many other like cases which occurred during the Tokugawa Shogunate show in what strict secrecy some parts of the laws were kept in those times.

The Taihō Code of 702, Jōyei-Shikimoku of 1232 and other old laws before the time of the Tokugawa Shogunate were printed and distributed *among officials* of the Imperial or the Shogunate Government, the governors of provinces, chiefs of clans etc., but they were not published in the sense in which laws are published in the present day. The Jōyei-Shikimoku, which was the fundamental Code during the time of the Hōjō-Regency, concludes with an oath by the councilors, to the effect, that they would render justice with impartiality, and according to reason, and in case of disobedience to the rules and principles set forth in the Code, they would incur the wrath and the punishment of the gods. These laws were all *commands addressed to the officials, not to the people. They were rules for the conduct of officials, not rules of conduct for the citizen.* It was upon officials only, that law imposed the obligation to observe the rules of law in their relation to the people, whether they acted in administrative or in judicial capacity. The people were merely passive objects of the law, and it was their part implicitly to obey the commands of officials. Austin and others, who define law as a command of the lawgiver, mean thereby a *command addressed to, and imposing obligations upon, the citizen.* But in Japan, *this conception was only reached after the introduction of Occidental jurisprudence* into the country. Two legislative acts in the beginning of the present reign very clearly show this transition in the nature of law. The publication of the new Criminal Code "Shin-ritsu-kōryō" in the 3rd year of Meiji marks the first step in the revolution of the legal idea. The policy of the Tokugawa

Government was based upon the famous Chinese maxim, "Let people abide by, but not be apprised of, the law." (民可使由之，不可使知之) and went so far as to keep the law in strict secrecy. Although the first Criminal Code was modeled upon Chinese Codes, the new Imperial Government took another and wiser Chinese maxim, "To kill without previous instruction is cruelty" (不教而殺虐也), and caused the new Code to be printed and published. I have said that the first Criminal Code was based upon the Chinese system and in the amended Code, the French Criminal Code was consulted. The comparison of the Imperial Proclamations which form the preambles to these two Codes is very interesting, as showing a great change in the conception of law, that took place during the three years, which intervened between the first and the second Code. In the Imperial Proclamation which is prefixed to the first Code, His Majesty enjoins his *officials to observe to rules of the Code;*

while in the Imperial Proclamation attached to the second Code, it is his *subjects as well as his officials* that are so commanded. In the same year with the publication of the second Code, that is 1873, a law was enacted (Ordinance 68, of the 6th year of Meiji), in which it was declared that "henceforth every law shall, on its promulgation, be posted up in convenient places during thirty days *for the information of the people.*" Since that time, several laws have been passed, in which the same principle is carried farther, and now the publication which is made in the Official Gazette has become an essential step in giving them binding force.

We have now reached the *third stage* in the evolution of the idea of law. At present, according to Art. 37 of the Constitution, every law requires the consent of both Houses of the Imperial Diet. Of the five Codes, which have been promulgated, the new Civil Code was the first which became law under the new constitutional government, and therefore, with the consent of the Diet.

From what I have said above, it will be seen that there are *three stages* observable in the development of the idea of law. At first, publication was not essential to the binding force of the law. Laws were commands addressed to the *magistrates*, not to the people. The people were merely the *passive object of the operation of the law.* Next comes an epoch, when the laws become commands addressed to the *people*, and publication forms an essential element of the law. People become the *direct object* of the law, and a party, as it were, to its operation. In the third and final stage, the people not only become a *party to the operation of the law*, but a *party to the making of it* through their representatives.

VIII

The Arrangement of the Code

The Civil Code drafted by Prof. Boissonade, which became law but never went into operation, was divided into the following Five Books; namely, Book I, "Persons"; Book II, "Property in General"; Book III, "Means of Acquiring Property"; Book IV, "Security of Rights *in* personam"; and Book V, "Evidence." The objections which were raised against this arrangement were many, some from scientific, others from practical, points of view; but it is needless to mention them here. Some will appear when I come to compare it with the arrangement of the new Code. The framers of the latter did not follow the arrangement of the first Code, nor did they adopt the classifications of the French or other codes based upon the Institutes of Justinian.

The new Civil Code is divided into the following Five Books, according to the plan which German jurists call "Pandekten-System": namely, Book I, "General Provisions"; Book II, "Rights *in rem*"; Book III, "Rights *in personam*"; Book IV, "Family"; and Book V, "Succession." One of the reasons for rejecting the so-called "Institutionen-System," and adopting the "Pandekten-System" was that the latter system of arrangement was peculiarly suited to the present state of law in Japan.

The first Code, following the French Code, had no distinct portion assigned to general rules applicable to all other parts. This system rendered frequent repetition of the same rules necessary in different parts of the Code, thereby making the whole work a voluminous code, containing 1762 articles; while the new Code, following the Saxon Civil Code and the then draft of the German Civil Code, placed at the beginning all the general rules, relating to persons as subjects of rights, to things as objects of rights, and to facts and events by which rights are acquired, lost or transferred. This method of arrangement avoided unnecessary repetitions and made the body of the law succinct; the new Code containing only 1146 articles.

The new Code, besides having a Book devoted to general provisions common to all legal relations, has distinct places set apart for the laws of Family and Succession. In the Code drafted by Prof. Boissonard, the law of family was included in Book I relating to "Persons," and the law of succession formed a part of Book III relating to the "Means of Acquiring Property." Now, this arrangement formed one of the strong reasons for postponing the operation of the first Code and reconstructing it on an entirely new basis.

Before the Restoration it was the *family*, and *not the individual*, that formed the unit of society. The family was then a corporation; and as a general rule, only the house-head could hold public office or private property, or transact business, all other members of the family being dependent upon him. But since the Restoration, this state of things has changed, and the disintegration of the family is rapidly going on. The family has now ceased to be a corporation in the eye of law, and the dependent members of the family or the house-members can hold office or property or transact business equally with its head. Japanese society is now passing *from the stage of family-unit to the stage of individual-unit.* But still, the family occupies an important place in the social life of the people, and there are many rules which are peculiar to their family relations, and which ought, on that account, to be grouped together and separated from the rules relating to persons regarded simply as individuals. The "Pandekten-System" is peculiarly suited to this transient state of society, for it provides for the rules relating to persons in their capacity as individuals or members of a society in the General Part, and sets apart a distinct place for those rules which relate to persons in their capacity as members of a family. In civilized societies, the rules which regard men as individuals belong to general law, while those which regard men in their family relations belong to particular law. But in less advanced communities, the case is just the reverse; the *family law may be said to form the general law*, the law relating to persons in their individual capacity falling under the category of *particular law*. Japan is now in a transition stage; so that the placing of the rules relating to individuals in the general part, and the rules relating to family relations in the particular part of the Code is, not only logically correct, but is especially suited to the present state of the Japanese law.

As to the place of the Succession Law in the Code, strong objection was raised against the arrangement of Prof. Boissonade which put it in Book III, under the head of "Means of Acquiring Property." In Japan, as I shall show presently, succession cannot, at least as regards the most usual kind of it, be regarded as a mode of acquiring property.

Comparative study of succession laws of different peoples in different degrees of civilization, shows that there are *three stages in the evolution* of this branch of law. In the first and earliest stage, succession is regarded as the mode of perpetuating the *worship* of ancestors; next comes the time when it is regarded as a mode of succeeding to the *status* of deceased persons; and it is only in the last stage, that succession becomes a mode of acquiring *property*.

Now in Japan, until recently, as the family was a corporation, the only person who could hold property was the head of a house. Consequently the only kind of succession which was then recognized by law was *katoku sōzoku* or the *succession to the headship of a house*, which was the succession to *status*, and the house-property descended to the heir as an appendage to the *status* of the house-headship. It is only after house-members were allowed to have independent property, that succession which can properly be said to be succession to property began to be recognized. So, there are, at present, two kinds of succession, *status-succession* and *property-succession* existing side by side. The status-succession cannot be put under the category of the law of property, nor can the property-succession be put under the law of persons. The arrangement of the "Pandekten-System," which devotes a particular Book to succession law at the end of the Code is peculiarly suited to this state of law, and recommended itself to the framers of the new Code in preference to the classification adopted by Prof. Boissonade.

IX

The Introduction of the Notion of Right

It will be seen, from what I have stated above, that the classification of rules in the new Civil Code is made upon the basis of *primary distinctions regarding rights*. But the notion of right did not originally exist in Japan, before the introduction of Western jurisprudence. Many Western writers assume that right is coeval with law, and law and right are only two terms expressing the same notion from different points of view. Some even go so far as to affirm, that right is anterior to law, and the latter only exists for the assurance or protection of the former. In Japan, however, the idea of right did not exist so long as her laws belonged to the Chinese Family. There was indeed the notion of *duty* or *obligation*, but neither the notion of right nor the word for it existed either in Japanese or Chinese. The nearest approach to it in Japanese was perhaps "*bun*" which means "*share*" or "*portion*." This word was frequently used to express the share or part which a person had in society and which he expected that society would recognize as his due. But this word was not quite definite in its meaning, and was more often used in a contrary sense, expressing a person's *duty*, or sometimes the *part* or *limit* which he ought not to exceed. So, when the notion of right was first introduced into Japan, there was no fit word to translate it, and a new word had to be coined to express this novel idea. The late Dr. M. Tsuda who had been sent to Holland by the Shogunate Government to study law in the University of Leyden, on his return to Japan published a book entitled "A Treatise on Western Public Law" in 1868, the year of the Restoration. In this book he used the new word "*ken-ri*" for right, which he coined by combining the words "*ken*" or "*power*" and "*ri*" or "*interest.*" This word has since been received to express the notion of right. Lord Avebury in his book "On the Origine of Civilization" (ch. VIII.) says that lower races are "deficient in the idea of right, though familiar with that of law," Sir Henry Maine says that "jus" among Roman lawyers generally meant not "a right" but "law"; and that Romans "constructed their memorable system without the help of the conception of legal right." I think it may be laid down as a general rule of the evolution of law, that *laws from being the rules of duty become the rules of right. Early laws impose duty but do not confer right.* But in the course of time, men begin to realize, that the benefit which results to any one on account of duty imposed upon another, is of greater importance than the duty itself; so that right which was at first only the *secondary notion* and nothing more than the reflection of duty, began to be regarded as the *primary* object of law. This change in the conception of law took place in Japan within the last forty years, and resulted in the classification of the rules of the Civil Code on the basis of right.

X

The Legal Position of Woman

With reference to Book I of the Code, which relates to "General Provisions," I will only touch upon the subjects of the *Legal Position of Woman* and that of *Foreigners*; for these are the two points where the Code has made greatest changes in that part of the law. I will first speak of woman.

Three periods may be distinguished in the history of Japan, as to the legal position of woman: the *first*, corresponding to the period during which our national law consisted solely of indigenous elements; the *second*, when Japanese law belonged to the Chinese Family of Law; and the *third*, dating from the time when our law passed from the Chinese to the European Family of law.

The first period extends from the beginning of our history to the introduction of Chinese civilization. During this period, woman seems to have occupied a higher place than in later times, filling positions of importance and honour in state, religion and household. Perhaps, the higher position, which woman occupied during the early period of our history, was due partly to the primitive simplicity and the absence of artificial doctrines, which later on assigned a subordinate position to woman. The first Imperial Ancestor and the central figure in national worship is a goddess Amaterasu O-mi-kami or the "Great Goddess of the Celestial Light." There was no law to prevent female members of the Imperial Family from ascending the throne, and there have been many Empresses who ruled the Empire. The Empress Jingō invaded and conquered Corea at the head of a large army.

With the conquest and subjugation of Corea by this "Empress of God-like Exploit" begins the second period in the history of the legal position of woman in Japan; for from this time, Chinese civilization began to enter Japan, first through Corea, and afterward from China directly. It was chiefly the doctrines of Chinese moral philosophy that changed the primitive state of comparative freedom and independence of woman, and placed her in an abnormally inferior position. The Chinese *doctrine of the perpetual obedience of woman* to the other sex is expressed in the precept of "the *three obediences*" (三從) :— "obedience, while yet unmarried, to a father; obedience, when married, to a husband; obedience, when widowed, to a son."

It is curious to note, by the way, that an exact counterpart of this doctrine of three obediences is to be found in Hindu Law. In one place Manu says: "Day and night women must be kept in dependence by the males of their family" (Manu IX. 2. Buehler's transl.); and in another place: "In childhood, a female must be subject to her father; in youth, to her husband; when her Lord is dead, to her sons." (v. 148).

Buddhism and Feudalism contributed to the keeping of woman in a state of dependence. Buddhism regards woman as an unclean creature, a temptation or snare to virtue and an obstacle to peace and holiness. Feudalism, which disdained anything effeminate, also regarded woman in the light of a temptation to courage and faithful performance of duty, and although she was treated with kindness and consideration far above that received in other Asiatic countries, she did not command that romantic homage which the gallant knights of Mediæval Europe paid to the other sex. Prof. Chamberlain, one of the best authorities on Japan, writes: — "Japanese feudalism — despite its general similarity to the feudalism of the West—knew nothing of gallantry. A Japanese knight performed his valiant deeds for no such fanciful reward as a lady's smile. He performed them out of loyalty to his lord, or filial piety towards the memory of his papa."

Thus, these three factors, Chinese philosophy,

Buddhism and Feudalism, combined to place the Japanese woman in a state of dependence during the second period. She could not become the head of a house; she could not hold property nor contract in her own name; she could not become a guardian of her own child; she could not adopt a child in her own name; in short, she had no independent *status* and was excluded from the enjoyment or exercise of almost all rights.

But in the third period, during which European civilization has been introduced, female education has spread throughout the country, Western jurisprudence has superseded Chinese, and Japanese law has become a member of the European Family of laws, a great revolution has come over the social and legal position of woman. This reform was consummated by the publication of the new Civil Code. This Code "created the new legal woman" as an able writer on Japan has expressed it. (Clement's Modern Japan. ch. VIII.) It proceeds upon the principle of equality of the sexes, and makes no distinction between man and woman in their enjoyment and exercise of private rights, so long as the woman remains single. She may now become the head of a house, in which case all house-members, whether male or female,—even her husband when she is married—come under her power and are legally dependent upon her. She may exercise parental authority over her own child, if her husband be dead. She may adopt children either alone, when she is single or a widow, or in conjunction with her husband, when married. She may make any contract, or acquire or dispose of property in her own name. In short, she may be a party to any legal transactions, as long as she remains *feme sole*. When she is married, her state of coverture obliges her to obtain the permission of her husband in doing certain acts, which may involve grave consequences upon their conjugal life; such as contracting debt, acquisition or loss of immovables or valuable movables, instituting legal proceedings, accepting or renouncing succession, entering into contract of personal service etc. Even in regard to these acts, she can not be considered as laboring under legal incapacity, for when she does these acts without her husband's permission, they are not void, but only voidable, that is, liable to be annulled by her husband (Civil Code, Art. 14.). With her husband's permission, she may also engage in business, in which case, she is considered in regard thereto as an independent person. (Civil Code, Art. 15.). That the Civil Code places husband and wife on an equal footing, except when consideration for their common domestic life requires some modifications, may be seen from the provision of Art. 17, which allows a wife to do the acts above mentioned, without the permission of her husband "when the interests of the husband and wife conflict," and also from the provision of Art. 790, in which it is stipulated that "a husband and wife are mutually bound to support and maintain each other."

The great revolution in the legal position of woman, which the new Civil Code brought about is nowhere so clearly seen, as in its regulations relating to the *property of married women.*

The laws relating to married women's property are different in different countries, and varies with the degree of civilization attained; but broadly, they may be grouped into the following *four systems* :—

(1) System of Conjugal Unity—In those systems of law, which regard man and wife as *one person,* or in which the wife's personality is merged in that of the husband, whatever the bride possesses at the time of marriage, becomes the property of the husband, as was the case in the English Common Law, or under the doctrine of *Manus* in the early Roman Law, or that of *Mund* in the early Germanic Law.

(2) System of Dowry.—Another system sets aside a part, at least, of the bride's fortune as a common conjugal fund, the management of which belongs to the husband, as was the case at one period under Roman Law, and under the Code Civil, and as is now practiced in the south of France.

(3) System of General Community of Conjugal Property.—This system exists under the Code Civil side by side with the dotal system, principally in the northern part of France.

(4) System of Separate Property.—Under this system marriage makes no change whatever in the property rights of the bride, as is the case in England since the Married Women's Property Act of 1882, and in many States of the United States.

Broadly speaking, the usual process in the evolution of the law of conjugal property is in the order which I have stated above, the system of unity corresponding to the lowest, and the system of separate property to the highest, scale of civilization. But in this respect, the compilers of the new Code have taken a decided step, and leaped, at one bound, *from the system of complete merger of wife's property in that of the husband to the system of separate property.* According to the Code (Art. 793—807), persons who are about to marry are allowed to make any contract with regard to their conjugal property, which will be binding upon them and can be set up against a third person, if registered before the registration of the marriage. If such contract be not made between them, their relations in regard to property are governed by the general rules of conjugal property, which, among others, lays down the fundamental rule, that the property belonging to a wife at the time of marriage or acquired after marriage in her own name, shall be her separate property. (Civil Code, Art. 807).

The reform in the Law of Divorce, which the new Civil Code made, also marks a great advance as regards the legal position of woman. During the second period, while the Japanese law belonged to the Chinese Family, the law of divorce was based upon the Chinese doctrine of "the Seven Grounds of Divorce" (七去) which are (1) sterility, (2) lewdness, (3) disobedience to father-in-law or mother-in-law, (4) loquacity, (5) larceny, (6) jealousy, and (7) bad disease. These grounds were adopted in the "House Law" (Koryō) of the Taihō Code. But it must be observed that these grounds were *not limitative*, as in the case of modern legislation. They are only mentioned as *just grounds for abandoning a wife*, or in some cases such as barrenness, adultery or hereditary disease, as a *moral obligation* which a husband owes to his ancestor to abandon the wife, because the object of marriage was the perpetuation of ancestor-worship, and barrenness may cause the failure of heir, adultery the confusion, and hereditary disease the pollution, of ancestral blood. (See my work on "Ancestor-worship and Japanese Law"). Practically, a wife could be divorced at the pleasure of her husband, under any slight or flimsy pretext, the most usual being that "she does not conform to the usage of the family." It must be further observed that divorce during this period meant only the abandonment of the wife on the part of the husband. The wife had no legal right to demand divorce from her husband on any ground. Divorce, therefore, was not a bilateral, nor even a reciprocal, act. It was an *unilateral act of the husband.* To bring an action against the husband, or to give information of a crime against him was itself considered a grave offence; and so a wife could not demand divorce in the court of law. Divorce was the privilege of the husband only, as in the Mosaic and other primitive laws.

But this state of things has changed since the Japanese law passed from the Chinese and entered the European Family of laws. In the 6th year of Meiji (1873) the following Law (No. 162) was enacted, which, for the first time, allowed the wife to bring an action of divorce against the husband:—"Whereas it has frequently happened that a wife asked divorce from her husband on account of unavoidable circumstances, to which the latter unreasonably withheld his consent for many years, thereby causing her to lose the opportunity of second marriage, and whereas this is an injury to her right of freedom, it shall be henceforth allowed to the wife to bring an action against her husband, with the assistance of her father, brother or other relative." This law may be considered a revolution in the legal position of woman. The new Civil Code went a step farther and placed husband and wife on an equal footing in this respect. According to the Code *two kinds of divorce* are recognized, *consensual* and *judicial*, the former being effected by arrangement of parties, while the latter is granted by a court of law on several grounds specified in Art. 813 of the Code. The grounds for judicial divorce include, inter alia, bigamy, adultery, sentence for an offence of grave nature, such cruel treatment or gross insult as make living together unbearable, desertion with evil intent, cruel treatment or gross insult of or by lineal ascendant, uncertainty, for a period of three years or more, whether the consort is alive or dead. Consensual divorce requiring the *consent of both parties* is a bilateral act, whereas divorce during the second period was an *unilateral act*, which took place at the will of the husband who gave her a "letter of divorce" formulated, as a custom, in three lines and a half "mikudari-han," stating that he gave her a dismissal, and nothing should henceforth stand in the way of her marrying again. As to the judicial divorce, either party to marriage can claim divorce from the other, if any of the grounds specified by law exists, so that husband and wife are now placed on an equal footing in this respect.

It will appear from the foregoing rough sketch of the three periods in the history of the law relating to the position of woman, that during the first period, while Shintoism was the only form of worship, woman held a higher place than in the second period, when Confucianism, combined with Buddhism and Feudalism held down woman in a state of subjection; while in the third era, a great revolution has been made in the position of woman, and equality with man, as far as her private rights are concerned, is vouchsafed to her under the new Civil Code.

XI

The Status of Foreigners

The possible forms, which the law of any country relating to the position of foreigners may assume, or the possible stages through which it may pass, may be arranged, by the broad generalization of comparative jurisprudence, under the *four* following heads :—

(1) Laws based upon the Principle of Enmity.

The laws of almost all barbarous peoples are based upon the principle that all foreigners are enemies, and consequently have no right whatever. Even after they cease to regard foreigners as enemies, they view their own laws as exclusively national, that is to say, they are applicable only to their own countrymen. Foreigners are, therefore, outlaws, and are placed outside the protection of the law.

(2) Laws based upon the Principle of Inferiority.

With the advance of civilization, especially

with the progress of commerce, foreigners are no longer regarded as enemies; but from disdain for foreigners, or from national egoism, they are placed in inferior position as regards the enjoyment of their private rights. Sometimes the enjoyment of many rights is totally denied them, or sometimes capricious limitations are placed upon their legal capacities. In this stage, foreigners enjoy private rights, but in a limited degree only.

(3) Laws based upon the Principle of Reciprocity.

Some countries make the conditions of foreigners dependent upon the treatment which their own people receive in other countries; and allow foreigners the enjoyment of their rights only so far as the countries of those foreigners allow their own people the same rights. This principle of reciprocity is adopted in France (Code Civil, Art. 11,), Austria (Das allg. buergerl. Gesetzbuch § 33.), Sweden, Norway, Servia and other countries.

(4) Laws based upon the Principle of Equality.

This is the most liberal and most advanced system of law relating to the legal condition of foreigners. Beginning in 1827 with the Dutch Civil Code, and followed by the Italian Civil Code of 1865, it has now been adopted in the majority of European and American States. They recognize the principle of equality as far as the enjoyment and exercise of private rights are concerned, some few exceptions only being usually made on grounds of national policy, such as the prohibition or limitation of the ownership of land or ships, the right of fishery, the right of working mines, or engaging in the coasting trade, and a few others.

Now, in regard to the legal condition of foreigners in Japan, we may distinguish *three periods*, which nearly correspond to the first, second and fourth stages above mentioned. The first period includes the time before the opening of the country to foreign intercourse; the second from that time until the new Civil

Code came into operation; and the third from that time till the present day.

During the first period, which may be called the *Period of Exclusion*, there was no intercourse with foreign countries. Foreigners were looked upon as barbarians or enemies. They could not come and reside in the country, except in a very few instances, and, therefore, they stood entirely outside the pale of the law.

The second period, which may be called *the Period of the Treaty Rights* begins from the date of the second visit of Commodore Perry in 1854 and the conclusion of the treaty of peace and amity by him, followed in 1858 by the first treaty of trade and commerce with the United States. Some ports were opened for foreign trade, and foreigners could come and reside within the limits of the treaty ports and engage in trade, business or missionary work. But their rights depended upon the *treaties, not upon the law of the country.* They enjoyed the privilege of extraterritoriality, that is to say, they brought their own laws with them, and remained under the jurisdiction of their respective consuls.

In the third period, which may be called the *Period of the Legal Rights,* foreigners enjoy their rights under the *law,* and the treaties only provide for the guarantees or limitations of rights. The new Civil Code, at its commencement, proclaims the noble principle of the equality of foreigners and native subjects before the law. Art. 2 provides that "foreigners enjoy private rights except in those cases where such enjoyment is prohibited by law, ordinance or treaty." And as to foreign juridical persons, Art. 36 provides, that "the existence of juridical persons other than states, administrative districts and commercial companies, is not admitted. But foreign juridical persons recognized as such by law or treaty do not come under this rule.

"Foreign juridical persons recognized as such

under the provision of the preceding paragraph have the same private rights as the same classes of juridical persons existing in Japan; but this does not apply to such rights as foreigners cannot enjoy, or so far as special provisions are made by law or treaty."

From the above provisions, it will be seen that the *new Civil Code made the equal enjoyment of rights a general rule*, and limitations and prohibitions exceptions. These limitations upon the foreigner's equal enjoyment of rights are not numerous, and do not differ greatly from those existing under the laws of many other modern states. Such restrictions are the ownership of Japanese ships, the right to work mines, to own shares in the Bank of Japan, the Yokohama Specie Bank or the Agricultural and Industrial Bank, to become members of the Stock Exchange, to engage in the emigration business, to receive bounties for navigation or ship-building and a few others. Otherwise foreigners are as free as the Japanese to engage in any commercial or industrial business, or to own shares in any Japanese companies. Until recently, the ownership of land was prohibited to foreigners, but this prohibition was abolished in 1910 on the principle of reciprocity. The first article of the Law relating to Foreigner's Right of Ownership of Land (the Law No. 51 of the 43rd year of Meiji) provides that "a foreigner resident or having domicil in Japan or a foreign juridical person registered in Japan is entitled to have ownership of land, if the law of his own country allows the ownership of land to Japanese subjects and Japanese juridical persons, provided that the foreign juridical person must obtain the permission of the Minister for Home Affairs before acquiring the ownership of land." Certain exceptions are made as to the lands in Hokkaidō, Taiwan, Kabafuto and in places specially pointed out by Imperial Ordinances as necessary to national defence. Even before the passing of the above law, foreigners could have the right of superficies, which is the right to use another person's land for the purpose of enjoying the right of property in structures and trees thereon. Moreover, the Law No. 39 of 1901, a right *in rem* called "the right of perpetual lease" was created especially for the benefit of foreign juridical persons, who had held land in the treaty ports under lease from the Japanese government. These leases which had been no more than rights *in personam* were turned into rights *in rem*, and *the rules relating to ownership are applied to them.* So, they are now practically the same as ownership; and as soon as they pass into the hands of Japanese subject they are turned into ownership.

It will appear from the foregoing statement that the condition of foreigners has undergone a great revolution during the half century which elapsed since the opening of the country to foreign trade. In the *first period*, foreigners had *no right* whatever; in the *second period*, they enjoyed their rights *under treaties;* but in the *third period*, that is, under the new Civil Code, they enjoy their rights *under the law*, which recognizes the principle of *equality* as far as private rights are concerned. Thus, in a comparatively short space of time, *Japanese laws passed from the stage of Enmity to that of Equality*—a revolution, which, in other countries, required many centuries to accomplish. The difference between the second stage in which their enjoyment of rights depended upon treaties, and the third stage in which their rights depend upon law, very clearly appeared during the war with Russia, as to the condition of Russians then resident in Japan. As the commercial treaties between Japan and Russia came to an end by the outbreak of the war, if Russian subjects had enjoyed their rights only under the treaties, they would not have been entitled to claim any protection from Japan, except as a matter of favour. But as their rights were now guaranteed by the provisions of the Code, Russian residents then remaining in Japan enjoyed the protection of law, just as peacefully as the citizens of any friendly states. The Code assures them the equal enjoyment of private rights, whether the country to which they belong be in amicable relations with Japan or not. This difference is further illustrated by Imperial Ordinance No. 352 of 1899, which declared foreigners who are not citizens of any of the Treaty Powers to have equal freedom of residence and profession with the subjects of the treaty Powers.

XII

The House and Kinship

It will be at once remarked by any one reading the new Civil Code that the Japanese family law, unlike that of Europe and America, rests upon the *double bases of House and Kinship*. The House or *iye*, in the sense in which it is employed in the Japanese law, does not mean a household, nor a dwelling place, but a group of persons, bearing the same surname, and subject to the authority of its chief who is called *koshu* or house-head. The other members who are subject to the authority of the house-head are called *kazoku* or house-members. It is not necessary that a house should consist of a group of persons, for a house may exist even when there is only one person in it, in which case that person is still called *koshu* or house-head. The house-membership consists of those relatives of the house-head or his predecessors, or sometimes also, of the relatives of house-members who are not related to the present or preceding house-heads by any tie of kinship, but who entered the house with the house-head's consent; such for instance, as the relatives of the house-head's adopted son, or daughter-in-law. (Civil Code, Art. 732—745). The persons who constitute the members of a house are defined by law, and a registry is kept, in each district, of persons who are in each house. The house-membership is constituted in accordance with the following rules.

1. A child enters the house of its father.
2. A child whose father is not known enters the house of its mother.
3. A *shoshi* or natural born child recognized by its father who is a house-member, or a natural-born child of a female member of a house enters the house of its father or mother, only when the house-head's consent is obtained.

4. A wife enters the house of her husband by marriage, except when a female house-head contracts a marriage, in which case the husband enters the house of his wife.

5. A relative of a house-head who is in another house or a relative of a house-member who has become such by adoption or marriage, enters the house, if the consent of the head both of the house he is leaving and of the house he is entering, is obtained. A person who can-not enter any house, such as a child whose parents can not be ascertained, establishes a new house, and becomes himself a house-head.

A house thus constituted is entered in the House-Registry or *koseki* which is kept in every district throughout the Empire.

Kinship, according to the Civil Code, arises from relationship by blood, by adoption or by marriage, and exists,

1. Between relatives by blood within six degrees inclusive.
2. Between husband and wife.
3. Between relatives by marriage within three degrees inclusive. (Civil Code, Art. 725).
4. Between an adopted child and adoptive parent and the latter's blood-relatives, the same relationship exists, from the date of the adoption, as that between blood relatives. (Civil Code, Art. 727).
5. Between step-parents and step-children, a wife and her husband's recognized child, the same relationship exists as that between parent and child.

Now, a house may include persons who are not the kindred of the house-head, because it includes the kindred of the preceding house-head, or the kindred of a house-member who is not related to the present house-head ; and may exclude even the nearest kindred, because, by adoption or marriage and other causes above mentioned, a man may enter another house, or return to the original house by the dissolution of the marriage or adoptive tie, or establish a new house, leaving his own parents or child in the original house. The *house, therefore, is wider than kinship on the one side, whilst it is narrower on the other.* Sir Henry Maine's description of ancient family so well tallys with the present state of the house in Japanese law—except in one particular which shows the peculiarity of Japanese family law,—that I cannot do better than quote his words in full.

"The family, then, is the type of an archaic society in all the modifications which it was capable of assuming ; but the family here spoken of is not exactly the family as understood by a modern. In order to reach the ancient conception, we must give to our modern ideas an important extension and an important limitation. We must look on the family as constantly enlarged by the absorption of strangers within its circle, and we must try to regard the fiction of adoption as so closely simulating the reality of kinship that neither law nor opinion makes the slightest difference between a real and an adoptive connexion. On the other hand, the persons theoretically amalgamated into a family by their common descent are practically held together by common obedience to their highest living ascendant, the father, grandfather, or great-grandfather. The patriarchal authority of a chieftain is as necessary an ingredient in the notion of the family group as the fact (or assumed fact) of its having sprung from his loins; and hence we must understand that if there be any persons who, however truly included in the brotherhood by virtue of their blood-relationship, have nevertheless *de facto* withdrawn themselves from the empire of its ruler, they are always, in the beginnings of law, considered as lost to the family. It is this patriarchal aggregate—the modern family thus cut down on one side and extended on the other—which meets us on the threshold of primitive jurisprudence." (Maine, Ancient Law, ch. v.).

Here I may conveniently compare the House in Japanese law with the Family in Roman Law, in order to show the characteristics of the former. It differs from the Roman family chiefly in the following points:—

(1) The House is not a family-group held together by "common obedience to the *highest living ascendant*" as in the Roman family, but is a *legal entity originally founded on ancestor-worship.* Therefore, it would be nearer the truth to say that it is by the common obedience to the *highest dead ascendant* that a house is held together. The house-head is not necessarily the highest living ascendant, but is a person who has *succeeded to the authority* of the highest ascendant. Sometimes, therefore, a son may be the house-head, and his father

may be a house-member under his authority, as in case of abdication of the house-headship, which I will explain presently. Or, sometimes, a nephew may be the house-head, and the uncle may be a house-member under him, as will happen, when a grandson succeeds to the grandfather by representation. Or again, there may be no relationship at all between the house-head and the house-member as I have explained above.

(2) In consequence of the difference above mentioned, the Roman family dissolved at the *death* of each paterfamilias, and each of the next highest ascendant became in his turn *sui juris* and a paterfamilias, having all his descendants in his power. Thus, if the deceased paterfamilias had three sons, there would be three families instead of one. But the Japanese house is never dissolved at the death or abdication of a house-head

and is succeeded by one person, all other members remaining *alieni juris* as before.

(3) According to the present Japanese law, *a woman may become a house-head*, and if she marries, she may continue to be the house-head and have her husband as a house-member under her power, provided such intention is expressed at the time of the marriage. (Civil Code, Art. 736.) Under the Roman Law, however, a woman could never exercise authority even over her children.

(4) According to the Roman Law, when a woman married, she always entered the husband's family and passed into the power of another; but according to the Japanese law the *husband enters the house of his wife* in case of the marriage of a female house-head, and also in case of the adoption of a son-in-law or "*muko-yōshi*," which I will explain later

on; so that the famous maxim of the Roman Law, "*Mulier est caput et finis familiae*"—a woman is the beginning and end of the family—does not apply to Japanese.

(5) Patria potestas was among the Romans an institution of *private law;* and it is so with us at the present time. But before the Restoration, it was an institution of public law as well as of private law, as I will explain when I come to speak of the decay of the house-system.

XIII

The House-Headship and the Parental Power

From the nature of the double bases of the Japanese Family Law, it follows that *a person may have two capacities,* one as a member of the legal house, and the other as a member of the wider group of kindred. Thus, a person may be a house-head or a house-member, and, at the same time, he may be a son. In such cases, if he is the son of a house-head, he is placed under the house-head's power and under the parental power of the same person; if he is a son of a house-member who is himself under the power of the house-head, he is under the power of two persons, the house-head and the father. But if the house-head is a minor, and his father or mother is a house-member, the former is under the parental power of the latter, while the latter is subject to the authority of the former. In such cases, conflict or inconvenience which may arise from mutual subjection to each other, is avoided by the provision of Art. 895 of the Civil Code, according to which the parent exercises the house-head's power on behalf of the minor house-head.

Of the two bases of the Japanese Family Law, the House and the Kindred, *more weight is always laid on the former than on the latter*, except in the two instances of the duties of support and maintenance and the succession to the property of house-members, both of which are new institutions introduced by the Code and are not bound by the limit of the house. In most other cases, the house takes precedence of the kindred, and a man's rights and duties, capacities and incapacities are usually determined by his position as a member of the house, and not by his position as a member of the kindred. *Parental power* which is based on the conception of kinship *is limited by the conception of the house,* and is recognized only so far as the parent and child are in the same house. So, if a son is not in the same house with his father or mother, he does not stand under the paternal power of either. The consent of the house-head is always necessary for the marriage, adoption, divorce or the dissolution of adoption of the house-member, but the consent of parents is only required *when the offspring is in the same house with them.*

Here again appears the difference between the Roman and Japanese family laws. The former recognizes only one authority of the head of the family, in the *patria potestas* of the highest male ascendant, and merged the parental power of the members of the family in that of the paterfamilias, while the Japanese law recognizes parental authority of the house-member side by side with the authority of the house-head. The authority of the house-head includes the right of consent above referred to, right of determining the residence of house-members, right of expelling them from the house or forbidding their return to it on certain grounds specified by the law, and the right of succeeding to the house-member's property in default of other heirs. The parental power includes the custody and education of children who are minors, right of correction, right of determining their place of abode, business or profession, of managing their property, or performing several legal acts on their behalf, subject in some cases to the approval of a family council. Most of the rights falling under the parental power *were formely included in the house-head's power*, but the Civil Code recognized the authority of parent and transferred them to the parental power, and greatly curtailed that of the house-head, only leaving those rights to him, which are necessary to the preservation and proper management of the house. This recognition by the Civil Code of the parental power besides the authority of the house-head shows the transient state of

Japanese society and is one of the points regarding which the framers of the new Code took pains to adjust the laws to the progressive tendencies of the society. Formerly, there was only one authority recognized by Japanese law, as in the case of the Roman Law—that of the house-head. But the new Civil Code took a decided step and recognized the parental power, besides the house-headship, due allowance being made to the long-existing custom among the people, by not going so far as to extend that recognition to the parents who belong to a different house from that of the child. The tendency of the laws of a progressive society must be the *gradual recognition of natural relationship in place of artificial connections*; and the process of evolution in this branch of law is *from House to Kinship*. The reform made by the new Civil Code may be regarded as the first step in that direction.

XIV

Relationship

The method of determining the degrees of relationship according to the new Civil Code is the same as that adopted in most countries of Europe and America, belonging to the system of Roman Law; that is, by reckoning the number of generations which intervene between two persons, either directly when they are lineal relatives, or through a common ancestor, when they are collaterals. This system of determining the degrees of relationship by the distance of consanguinity is the most natural one and is, for that reason, adopted from Western jurisprudence by the framers of the Code. But, previous to the adoption of the Code, while Japanese law still belonged to the Family of Chinese Law, relationship was determined in a different way. The basis of the new system is *the distance of blood-relationship* between relatives; but the old law rested on the *double bases of blood-relationship and family rank*, that is to say, the degree of relationship was determined not only by the distance of blood-relationship, real or fictitious, but also by the consideration of *superiority* or *inferiority* of their relative positions in the family. In "the Ceremony Law," or "Gi-sei-ryō" (儀制令) of the Taihō Code (701 A.D.), kindred are divided into the following Five Ranks or "Go-tō-shin."

(1) The Relatives of First Rank are: father and mother, adoptive father and adoptive mother, husband, son and daughter.

(2) The Relatives of the Second Rank are: grandfather and grandmother, *tekibo* (wife of the father of a concubine's child), step-mother, uncle and aunt, brothers and sisters, husband's parents, wife and concubine, brother's child, grandson and granddaughter, and son's wife.

(3) The Relatives of the Third Rank are: great grandfather and great grandmother, uncle's wife, husband's nephew, cousin, brother and sister by half-blood on father's side, husband's grandfather and grandmother, husband's uncle and aunt, wife of nephew, step-father, and child of husband by his former wife or concubine, provided the child is living in the same house.

(4) The Relatives of the Fourth Rank are: great great grandfather and great great grandmother, grandfather's brother and sister, father's cousin, husband's brother and sister, brother's wife and concubine, second cousin, grandfather and grandmother on mother's side, uncle and aunt on mother's side, brother's grandchild, cousin german's child, sister's child, great grandchild, grandson's wife and concubine and child of wife's or concubine's former consort.

(5) The Relatives of the Fifth Rank are: parents of wife or concubine, aunt's child, cousin on mother's side, great great grandchild, grandchild by a daughter who entered another house by marriage, and son-in-law.

The above table shows that the degree of relationship was greatly modified by the consideration of rank in the family; so that those who stand in the same rank are not always related in an equal degree, when measured only with reference to the distance of consanguinity. It will be seen that *precedence is generally given to father's and husband's relatives, and to those who are in the same house, in preference to mother's and wife's relatives and to those who are in another house.* Thus, uncle and aunt on the father's side stand in the Second Rank, while those on the mother's side stand in the Fourth. Husband is the relative of the First Rank to wife, but the wife is the relative of the Second Rank to the husband. Husband's parents are in the Second Rank, while wife's parents are in the Fifth. Nephew and niece by brother are in the Second Rank, while those by sister are in the Fourth. Grandchild by son is in the Second, while grandchild by daughter is in the Fifth Rank, because the latter is in another house on account of marriage.

The law also made distinction between *sonzoku* or "superior kin" and *hizoku* or "inferior kin." The former includes all relatives, lineal and collateral, who stand above any person in the same lateral line of the table of consanguinity; such as father, uncle, father's cousin, grandfather etc., while the latter includes those who stand in the lateral lines below him, such as son, nephew, cousin's child, grandson etc.

This system of classifying relatives into Five Ranks was derived from the *Chinese Law of Mourning*. From ancient times down to the present day, Chinese law has been very strict as to mourning, because it was considered as the highest duty of a man to show respect and love toward the departed soul of his relative by that act; and the moral as well as the legal code prescribed even the "Mourning of Three Years" to a dutiful son. Chinese codes abound in minute regulations as to the mourning dress, the duration of the time of mourning and the conduct of mourners. The *mourning dress is divided into five classes* and the duration of the period of mourning is fixed by the class of the mourning dress which the mourner ought to wear. The mourning dress is coarser in material and make, as the person mourned for stands nearer and higher in the family position to the mourner; the first class which is worn for parents, husband, and husband's parents, being the coarsest. The first class mourning dress is worn for three years, the second for two years, the third for nine months, the fourth for five months and the fifth for three months. Relatives are classified *according to the five classes of mourning dresses* which are worn for them. Thus, for instance father and mother belong to the relative of the first class mourning dress; grandparents to the second class; cousins to the third; great uncles and aunts to the fourth; and wife's parents to the fifth. This *classification of relatives according to the five classes of mourning dresses very nearly corresponds to the Five Ranks mentioned in the Taihō Code*, except with respect to great grandparents and great great grandparents, who belong to the Third and Fourth Rank respectively according to the Taihō Code, but who are placed according to Chinese law in the second class. Besides, this classification which is made in the Ceremonial Law of the Chinese Codes, finds its place in the "Ceremony Law" of the Taihō Code, instead of the "House Law" where one would naturally expect to find it. So, there is little room for doubt, that the above-mentioned *Japanese classification of the relatives into the "Five Ranks" had its origin in the Chinese law of mourning dress.*

During the Tokugawa Shogunate, the study of Chinese classics was greatly encouraged, and in 1638 the famous "Bukki-ryō" (服忌令) or the "Mourning Law," was made, which has since been amended several times and the classification of the "Five Ranks" went practically into disuse, until it was revised by the Criminal Code of 1870, which struck off concubines from the Third, Fourth and Fifth Ranks, and made a few other unimportant alterations. But with the publication of the present Criminal Code in 1882, it was abolished, and was replaced sixteen years later, by the present system of reckoning relationship adopted in the new Civil Code. In this respect too, Japanese law has passed from the Chinese to the European Family of law.

XV

The Law of Personal Registration and the Civil Code

As the house in the Japanese Family Law is narrower, in one respect, than kindred, and may exclude even the nearest relatives by blood, and wider, in another respect, and may include strangers, there is no logical test to determine the sphere of persons constituting the house other than their common subjection to the authority of one man, the house-head. Some other *external legal evidence* is required, therefore, for determining the constituent of a particular house. Such evidence is supplied by the *register* which is kept in every district throughout the Empire. As a person's birth, marriage, adoption, guardianship, death, succession, entrance to, or separation from, a house, acquisition or loss of nationality, and every other change of man's status are recorded in the register, the law relating to registration forms a supplementary law to the Civil Code and the present law was promulgated and put into force on the same day as the Code. As the register is the record of man's legal position in society, the development of society is often reflected in the law of registration. *Three stages* may be distinguished in the history of the law of personal registration in Japan: (1) the *Epoch of Clan-registration;* (2) the *Epoch of House-registration;* and (3) the *Epoch of Status-registration.* These epochs show the changes in the units of state and correspond to the three stages in the process of social disintegration.

In the early days of Japanese history, it was not the individual nor the family that formed the unit of state. The state only took cognizance of *clans* and the government of families and individuals in each clan was left to the chief of the clan or *uji-no-kami* who was usually the eldest male descendant of an eponymous ancestor. He was honored and obeyed by clansmen as the representative of their common ancestor. He was the head of their worship, their leader in time of war, and their governor in time of peace. There were Great Clans or *ō-uji* and Small Clans or *ko-uji*, the latter being included in the former. Clansmen of the Small Clan were governed by their chief who was himself subject to the chief of the Great Clan. The Emperor was the supreme authority over them, and all the laws and proclamations of the Imperial Government were transmitted to the *uji-no-kami* of the Great Clans, who, in turn, transmitted them to the *uji-no-kami* of the Small Clans. Thus each clan was a body founded on community of blood and worship and *formed an administrative division of the country*, corresponding to the present administrative divisions, such as provinces, cities, towns, districts and villages

Since the introduction of Chinese civilization

and the Reform of the Taika Era (645 A.D.), in spite of the fact that the clan-system of government continued for a long time afterward, the basis of the administrative division of the country gradually changed from a *personal* to a *territorial system* and provinces and districts took the place of clans.

In those early days of clan-government, it was of the utmost importance that each man's clan-name should be kept sacred. As only those who belonged to certain clans could fill high official positions, or join the Imperial body-guard, and as several other privileges were enjoyed by particular clans, attempts were often made by clansmen to forsake their original clans and surreptitiously adopt the names of other and more influential clans. In order to put a stop to these abuses; the "ordeal of hot water" or *kugadachi* was resorted to, which consisted in plunging the hand into hot water before the temple of a god. It was claimed that those who assumed false clan-names would suffer injury, while the innocent would escape unhurt. Afterward, in the year 815 A.D., a "Register of Clan-names" or the Shōji-roku was compiled, a part of which is still in existence to-day. This Register consisted of 30 volumes and contained 1182 clan-names.

The introduction of the House-register or *ko-seki* dates back as far as the first year of the Taika Era. But it owes its origin to the adoption of Chinese institutions, and although its introduction was earlier in date than the final compilation of the register of clan-names, its historical order must come after that of the Clan-Registry, for the system of House-Registry has continued from that remote period down to the present time.

It was only in the year of the publication of the new Civil Code (1898), that our law of registration began to enter upon the third stage of its development. The present law, which was promulgated at the same time as the Civil Code, and which replaced the previous law of 1871 still retains the name of "Koseki Hō" or the "Law of House-Registration"; but *the character of the law has undergone a change*, necessitated by the progress of the social condition of the country, for it provides for the *registration of individual status or "mibun-tōki" as well as of house registration.*

It is sometimes asserted that the family was the original unit of the state, and that an aggregation of families formed a clan. But *this view seems to reverse the real order of development.* The clan grew out of the expansion of a family, and separate households grew up within the clan by the increase of clansmen. It was their common worship and common clan-name which united them to a group. So it was the clan which was first recognized by the state and formed its unit. The family or house was included in the clan and did not yet possess separate existence in the eye of the law. It *was only by the gradual disintegration of the clan and the growth of the central power of the state that the family or house came to the fore, and began to form the unit of the state. Thus, the constituent elements of each society become smaller and smaller, until they divide themselves into atoms or individuals.*

XVI

Adoption

The importance of the fiction of adoption to primitive society has been illustrated by Sir Henry Maine in many places. In one passage, he says, "Without the fiction of Adoption which permits the family tie to be artificially created, it is difficult to understand how society would ever have escaped from its swaddling-clothes, and taken its first step towards civilization" (Ancient Law ch. II.) Its importance in India and also at Rome and Athens is well known among students of historical and comparative jurisprudence. But in modern systems of law, adoption no longer occupies the position of importance which it held in archaic societies. It still survives in most of the countries which have received Roman Law, but with several restrictions as to its effects, which make it in no way resemble that assumption of real kinship which characterized the ancient form of adoption. To the English Family of law, it is totally unknown as a legal institution.

But in Japan, adoption may be regarded as the corner-stone of Family Law. Without it, the continuity of the House, upon which rests the perpetuation of ancestor-worship, cannot be maintained. The practice of adoption has been so common and universal among the people, from ancient times down to the present day, that Prof. Chamberlain writes "it is strange, but true that you may often go into a Japanese family and find half-a-dozen persons calling each other parent and child, brother and sister, uncle and nephew, and yet being really either no blood-relations at all, or else relations in quite different degrees from those conventionally assumed." ("Things Japanese.")

Adoption in different systems of law *may be classified with regard to its object, under the following four heads:—*

(1) Adoption for the purpose of perpetuating *the family worship.*

(2) Adoption for the purpose of obtaining a *successor to house-headship.*

(3) Adoption for the purpose of obtaining a *successor to property.*

(4) Adoption for *charitable purposes, or for consolation in case of childless marriage.*

The historical order of the development, or rather the decay, of the law of adoption is usually as indicated above. I will proceed to explain them in order.

(1) Adoption for the purpose of perpetuating *family worship.*

Death without an heir to perpetuate the worship of ancestors was considered to be the greatest act of impiety which a descendant could commit. So, in the case of the failure of male issue, it was the *bounden duty* of a house-head to acquire a son by means of adoption. Adoption was, as Fustel de Coulanges says, "a final resource to escape the much dreaded misfortune of the extinction of a worship."

Many provisions of our ancient Code show that the object of adoption was the perpetuation of the ancestral cult. The House Law of the Taihō Code provides that "a person *having no child* may adopt one from among his relatives *within the Fourth Rank of Kinship*, whose age does not exceed that which might have been attained by a son of the adopter's own body." According to some commentators on the Taihō Code, "having no child" here means that the adoptive father should have reached the age of *sixty*, or the adoptive mother *fifty*, without having *male issue*. The reason for *limiting the age of the adopter*, was, that as long as any hope of having a male issue of blood, that is, the direct descendant of his ancestors, existed, the head of a house should not permit a person of more distant relationship to become the successor to the *sacra*.

That the object of adoption was the perpetuation of ancestor-worship may also be inferred from the old strict rule that only a *kinsman could be adopted as a son*. The Taihō Code did not permit adoption of kindred beyond the *Fourth Rank*, as I have said above. From the remains of the Taihō Criminal Code which have come down to us, we know that a punishment of one year's penal servitude was inflicted upon one who adopted a son from a different clan. This prohibition against the adoption of a person not related by blood derives its origin from the belief, which generally exists where the practice of ancestor-worship prevails, that "*the spirit does not receive the offerings of strangers*."

Another requirement of adoption, which is to be found in the laws of many countries, is the absolute *failure of male issue*. The House Law of the Taihō Code allowed adoption only in case a man had no son. The object of this rule is clear from what I have said above. A remoter relative should not be admitted where there is a nearer descendant to make offerings.

There is one peculiar form of adoption called *muko-yōshi* or "adoption of son-in-law," the origin of which must be attributed to the same cause. As I have said above, the law considered a man *childless*, even though he had a daughter. Males were the only continuators of worship. Those who had daughters only were, therefore, obliged to adopt a son; but it was necessary for the blood of the ancestor to be, if possible, *continued in the house.* In such cases, a house-head selects a person who is fit to be his daughter's husband and adopts him as a son. If adoption and marriage take place at the same time, it is called *muko-yōshi* or "adoption of son-in-law." The same object may also be attained by the subsequent marriage of the adopted son with the daughter of the adopter, for the collateral relationship of brother and sister *by adoption* is no bar to their marriage.

(2) Adoption for the purpose of obtaining a *successor to house-headship*.

As the house is the seat of ancestor-worship and the house-head is the continuator of the *sacra*, this kind of adoption cannot be regarded as differing from that above mentioned. But with the development of the house-system, the authority of the head of a house began to be regarded as a distinct object of inheritance by itself and the family *sacra* only as one of the duties incumbent upon the house-head. Especially was this the case, when hereditary office, profession or fief belonged to house-headship. In Japan, this stage was reached when the Feudal System was established, and *Daimios* and *Samurais* had their fiefs belonging to their houses. Under the Feudal régime, *the nature of military service required that males only should become house-heads.* Hence the failure of male issue was the cause of adoption. It was necessary to make provision against the contingency of a house becoming extinct and the fief being escheated by failure of an heir. As professions were at that time usually hereditary and were considered as belonging to certain houses, adoption was frequently resorted to, in *order to keep the profession in the house*. Physicians, artists, masters of fencing, riding, archery, professors of classics and the like often adopted, by special permission, those qualified to succeed them in the profession, even though they may have had sons of their own, the latter, however, being unworthy of their fathers. This kind of adoption was called *geidō-yōshi* or "arts-adoption."

It has just been remarked that the Taihō Code fixed the lower limit of the adopter's age at sixty for the father and fifty for the mother. But this rule took another form under the law of the Tokugawa Government. The limit of the age was fixed as low as *seventeen*. A house-head above that age, or even by special permission under that age, who had no male issue was allowed to adopt a son, in order to prevent the extinction of a house by his sudden death, causing the escheat of his feudal property. A person between the ages of seventeen and fifty years could adopt a son even on his death-bed, which kind of adoption was called *kiu-yōshi* or "quick adoption." But after the age of fifty, "quick adoption" was not allowed, so that he was obliged to provide for the succession to the house-headship early in life, even if he still had the hope of having male issue. The Taihō Code allowed adoption only in old age, because it was desirable that ancestor-worship should be continued by the nearest blood descendants. The Tokugawa Law allowed and encouraged adoption by young people, and attached severe penalties to the neglect of the precaution to provide for succession early in life, in order to avoid the chance of a house becoming extinct.

(3) Adoption for the purpose of obtaining a *successor to property*.

Next comes the time when the notions of

succession to the house-cult and house-headship gradually recede into the background and the notion of property succession comes to the fore. This stage is first reached in the new Civil Code. With the Restoration of the Imperial power and the abolition of Feudalism, house-headship has lost more than half of its former importance. Fiefs were abolished; offices and professions ceased to be hereditary privileges of house-heads; and, so far as public law is concerned, house-members now stand on an equal footing with house-heads. What remains of the rights and privileges attaching to house-heads is enjoyed within the sphere of private law. Of these the right of enjoying house-property is the most important, at least, so far as material interests are concerned. Besides, house-members are now allowed to have independent property of their own, as I have already explained, and they may adopt just in the same way as house-heads, provided the consent of the latter is obtained. (Civil

Code, Art. 750). During the Feudal period, only house-heads were allowed to adopt, because the object of adoption was the continuation of house-headship; but now *adoption is no longer the exclusive privilege of house-heads*, because its object is not limited to obtaining a successor to house-headship. Wills, although not quite unknown to the old Japanese law, were very rare in practice, and their place was taken by adoption. *What is done in Europe and America by will is done in Japan by adoption.* Instead of giving away property to another person by will, which becomes effective after death, a Japanese takes another person into his house by adoption during his lifetime and makes the latter the expectant successor to his property.

(4) Adoption for *consolation in case of childless marriage.*

This is the only kind of adoption which has no connection with the house-system and marks the last stage in the history of the law of adoption. In Occidental systems of jurisprudence, will has taken the place of adoption, and the principal ground on which this institution is still retained is for *consolation in case of childless marriage.* Although the adopted child usually obtains the right of succeeding to the adopter's property, this is the effect of adoption and cannot be regarded as the ground for allowing adoption. Consolation in the case of a childless marriage constitutes the principal motive to this act, and therefore most systems allow adoption only when the adopter has no child of his own and is of such an age as to preclude reasonable expectation of any being born to him. In Japan also, adoption often takes place from the same motive, but it cannot be regarded as a legal ground, because the new Civil Code does not limit adoption to the case of childless marriage. The Japanese law of adoption is now in a transient state, and *is passing from the second to the third stage of its development, but has not yet entered the fourth, nor has it yet passed out of the first.*

XVII

Succession in General—The Evolution of the Law of Succession

I think it may be laid down as a universal rule of the evolution of the law of succession that it passes through *three stages of evolution:* the *first stage is that of the succession to sacra,* the *second that of the succession to status* and the *third that of the succession to property.* Each stage of development, however, did not form a distinct period in itself, but the later was gradually evolved out of the earlier by the process of differentiation. In ancient times, the duty of performing and continuing the *worship* rested on the head of a house, and the property of a house belonged exclusively to him. He exercised authority over the members of his house, because he was the *continuator of the ancestral sacra,* and, in one sense, the representative of the ancestor. He owned his property, because it was left by the ancestor. The *authority and property of a house-head rested on the worship of ancestors.* In those times, continuation of house-worship formed the sole object of inheritance. But in the course of time, the authority of the house-head which at first comprehended both power over the members of the house and rights over house property, came to be considered by itself in law. Afterwards the two constituent elements of the authority of the house-head gradually began to be separately considered, until, at last, *property came to be regarded as a distinct object of inheritance.*

There are perhaps few systems of law which can illustrate the above proposition and indicate the process of gradual development so clearly as the Japanese law of succession to the headship of a house. In the Succession Law or "Keishi-ryō" of the Taihō-Code (701 A.D.), there is a provision that if a presumptive heir of a noble family "is not fit to succeed to the important duty" owing to the committal of crime or to disease, he may be disinherited and another presumptive heir may be substituted. The official commentary on this Code "Ryō-no-gigé" says "*to succeed to the important duty*" means "to succeed a father and *inherit the sacra*, for the matter of worship is the most important." It appears that, at this time, the continuation of ancestor-worship was the principal object of succession. Since the Middle Ages, the word *katoku sōzoku* or "the succession to house-authority" was used for succession, and in the Feudal period, especially during the Tokugawa Shōgunate, succession represented the continuity of the *status of house-headship*. In later times, *katoku* which literally means *house-authority* was very frequently used for *house-property* which formed the object of inheritance just as the word "familia" in Roman law was often used to designate property. This transition of the use of the word *katoku* indicates that the law of succession was gradually passing from the second to the third stage referred to.

The present law of succession, contained in Book V of the Civil Code, shows that *Japanese law is rapidly passing from the second to the third stage above mentioned, without losing its original trait of the suceession to sacra.* The new Civil Code recognizes *two kinds* of succession ; *succession to house-headship* or *katoku sōzoku* and *succession to property* or *isan sōzoku.* But there are many rules still remaining, which show that the foundation of the succession to the house-headship is the necessity of continuing the worship of ancestors. Article 987 contains the following provision :—

"The ownership of the records of the genealogy of the house, of the articles used for house-worship and of the family tombs, constitutes the special rights of succession to the headship of a house."

This important provision means that those

things which are specified therein form the special objects of inheritance. They cannot be bequeathed away, nor can they be seized for debt.

Though the house is no longer a corporation, as was formerly the case, it is still a legal entity whose continuance is assured by law, and does not break up at the death of each house-head. So, there can be only one heir to its headship; and new Civil Code recognizes many kinds of heirs to house-headship in order to provide against the contingency of the failure of the heir. They are: (1) the Legal Heir, (2) the Appointed Heir, (3) the Chosen Heir, and (4) the Ascendant Heir. The Legal Heir who comes first in the order of succession, *is the lineal descendant of a househead, who is at the same time a member of his house.* Among lineal descendants, the nearer are preferred to the remoter, males to females, and legitimate children to illegitimate, seniors in age being always accorded priority when they are equal in other respects (Civil Code, Art. 970). Modern writers on law usually give as a reason for the preference of nearer to remoter kinsmen that the order of succession is determined by the *degree of affection* which the deceased is presumed to have entertained towards his relatives, and also by the presumed intention of the person who dies intestate as to the disposition of his property. For the preference of males over females *feudal reasons* are often given. These reasons also form the principal basis of our present law. But, the reasons for the *existence* of the rule and its *origin* are not always the same. Originally, the *nearest in blood to the ancestors worshipped*, and his male descendants were preferred, because they were considered to be the fittest persons to offer sacrifices to the spirits of ancestors.

The Legal Heir is *heres necessarius* and is not allowed to renounce the succession, whilst other kinds of heirs are at liberty to accept or renounce the inheritance. It is the bounden duty of a descendant who is the Legal Heir to accept the inheritance and continue the *sacra* of the house.

The house-head cannot bequeath away from him more than one half of the property (Civil Code, Art. 1130), nor can he disinherit him, unless there exists one of the grounds mentioned in Art. 975 of the Civil Code. The causes especially mentioned there are:—

(1) ill-treatment or gross insult to the house-head, (2) unfitness for house-headship on account of bodily or mental infirmities, (3) sentence to punishment for an offence of a nature disgraceful to the name of the house and (4) interdiction as a spendthrift. These grounds relate directly to the house-head's authority and indirectly to ancestor-worship and the necessity of maintaining intact the reputation and property of the house.

In case there is no legal presumptive heir to a house-head, he may appoint an heir, either in his lifetime or by his will (Civil Code, Art. 979).

If, at the time of the death of a house-head, there is neither a Legal Heir, nor an Appointed Heir, the father of the deceased, or if there is no father, or if he is unable to express his intention, the mother, or, if there are no parents, or both are unable to express their intention, the family council, chooses an heir from among the members of the house according to the following order:—first, the surviving wife, if she is a "*house-daughter*"; secondly, brothers; thirdly, sisters; fourthly, the surviving wife who *is not a* "*house-daughter*"; and lastly, the lineal descendants of brothers and sisters (Civil Code, Art. 982).

Now, in this also, the desire for preserving the blood of ancestors will be seen from the order in which the heir is chosen. The surviving consort of the last house-head comes *first* in the order of succession, provided that she is a "*house-daughter*," but *fourth* if she is not the descendant in blood of an ancestor of the house.

If there is neither a Legal, nor an Appointed, nor a Chosen, Heir, then the nearest lineal ascendant of the last house-head succeeds, males being always preferred to females between persons standing in the same degree of relationship (Civil Code, Art. 984).

If there are no other heirs above mentioned, the family council must choose one from among other relatives of the last house-head or members of his house, house-heads of branch-houses or members of the principal-house or branch-houses. If none of the persons above mentioned be existing or able to succeed, then as a last resort, the family council may choose an heir from among other persons (Civil Code, Art. 985).

From the foregoing enumeration of the various kinds of heirs, it will be seen that the law takes every precaution against the contingency of a house becoming extinct; for with the extinction of the house, the worship of its ancestors would come to an end.

XVIII

Property Succession.—The Recognition of House-member's Separate Property

The second kind of succession, namely Property Succession is a new institution introduced by the new Civil Code. According to the Code, *Property Succession includes only the succession to the property of a house-member on his death.*

Before the Restoration of 1868 a house was in a strict sense a corporation, and a house-member could not have separate property of his own. All he gained he gained for the house-head, or rather for the house; all he possessed or enjoyed he possessed or enjoyed, by the license of the house-head, not as of right. No question of succession to the property of house-members could therefore arise at that time. But the Restoration completely changed this state of things. It was one of the policies of the new Imperial Government to appoint its officials not, as before, on account of birth, but on account of personal merits, no distinction whatever being made as to whether they were house-heads or house-members. Formerly, it was only the house-head that could hold public office. During the first years of the Imperial Government, statesmen and soldiers who had served in the cause of the Restoration were rewarded with life or perpetual annuities. But many of them were not house-heads; some were *inkyo* or house-members who had become such by abdicating house-headship, others were younger members of houses. Now, *these annuities and the salaries of civil and military officials being given by the State for personal service or merits, could not be treated as house-property. Thus began the independent and separate property of house-members,*— the first great blow which the old family system received at the hand of the Imperial

Government. It is interesting to note that this is exactly what happened in the beginning of the Roman Empire, when *castrense peculium* of filiusfamilias was recognized for military services, and three centuries afterward *quasi-castrense peculium* for civil services.

The issue of a law in 1872, which abolished the prohibition of sale of land, and *granted title-deeds to landowners*, the issue, in the following year, of the *government bonds* for public loans, and the *establishment of joint-stock companies and savings-banks* mark the next step in the development of the separate property of house-members. The courts of law began to recognize house-members' separate property in the title-deeds, bonds, stocks, debentures or savings which they held in their own names, and thus *individual property began to grow up by the side of house-property*. But on the other hand, a Law (No. 275) was passed in 1872 to the effect, that the house-head should not be liable for the debt contracted by house-members, unless he became a surety to the contract.

Although the separate property of house-members was thus established, the rule of succession was not settled until the promulgation of the new Civil Code. As a rule, the property left by a deceased house-member went to the house-head. But here again, the Code took a decided step. It gives the right of succession to the *nearest descendants equally, whether they are males or females, or whether they are in the same house with the deceased or not,* the right of representation being always given to the children of predeceased descendant. After descendants comes the surviving consort; next in order, the lineal ascendant; and *as the last successor, the house-head.* Other rules relating to this kind of succession do not differ much from those we find in Western countries.

By comparing the two kinds of succession, above mentioned, we shall notice that they present a remarkable contrast and indicate the transient stage in which the Japanese law of succession finds itself. The rules relating to succession to house-headship rest chiefly upon indigenous elements, while those relating to succession to property are based principally upon Western ideas.

XIX

Succession inter vivos

Another characteristic of the Japanese succession law is the existence of Succession *inter vivos,* side by side with Succession *mortis causa.* The succession which arises during the lifetime of the person succeeded, takes place only with reference to *succession to house-headship;* for house-headship may come to an end either by *a house-head's death or the loss of house-headship during his life-time.* Successsion *inter vivos* takes place in the following cases :—

i. *Inkyo* or abdication of house-headship.
ii. Loss of nationality by a house-head.
iii. Marriage of a female house-head.
iv. Divorce of a husband who has married a female house-head.
v. When a house-head leaves the house in

consequence of the invalidation of his marriage or adoption.

I will explain each of the causes of succession *inter vivos* in order.

i. *Inkyo* or abdication of house-headship.

House-headship is not a lifelong authority. It may be lost in several ways during lifetime, the most usual of which is its abdication or *inkyo* which literally means "*living in retirement.*" The origin of this custom has been sometimes ascribed to Buddhism, but I have shown in a work especially devoted to this subject ("Inkyo-ron" or "Treatise on Abdication" 1891) that this institution was originally derived from China, and developed among us by the influence of Buddhism and Feudalism. The abdication of house-headship may be classified with reference to its *causes* under the following *four heads*: namely, (1) Religious Abdication, (2) Political Abdication, (3) Judicial Abdication, and (4) Physiological Abdication.

(1) Religious Abdication.

After the introduction of Buddhism, the practice gradually grew up, among higher classes, of withdrawing from active life when any person attained "the age of retirement," which was *seventy* according to the Chinese Ritual Code, the Li Chi (禮記), and closing his days in religious devotion as a hermit or priest. Our history abounds in instances where ministers of state tendered their resignations for the purpose of devoting the rest of their lives to religious practice. As I have already said, house-headship was rather an institution of public law than of private law, and the *resignation of office usually brought with it the loss of house-headship*. In the later times, the middle and lower classes began to imitate the examples set by the heads of noble families, until it has become a general custom among the people. Until recently, it was a very common practice for retired persons to shave their heads, like Buddhist priests, in token of their having given up secular business and of having embraced the religious life. It was for this reason that the designation of *nyūdō-inkyo* or "priestly retirement" was employed for this kinds af abdication.

This practice is very common among the Hindu, whose life is distributed into three periods; namely, the Student, Householder and Ascetic periods. Minute regulations as to the life of the ascetic are contained in Hindu law books, especially in the sixth chapter of the Code of Manu. Entering into a monastery seems to have had the same effect as death in the early Germanic and English laws (Young's Anglo-saxon Family Law; Co. Litt. 133; Blaxland's Codex Legum Anglicanarum p. 217) and in the French law before the Revolution (Zachariae, Franz. Civilrecht § 162), but since the abolition of civil death in modern legal systems succession *inter vivos* does not occur in the European Families of laws.

(2) Political Abdication.

From an early period of our history, it was very common for the upper and middle classes to resort to abdication for various political reasons. Sometimes it was made use of by unscrupulous minister of State or influential retainers of *Daimios* to deprive masters of their power, and put other persons, perhaps puppets, in their places; sometimes, house-heads retired in order to shift responsibilities to other persons' shoulders, and wield real power themselves, or pull strings from behind the curtain; or sometimes they gave up the worldly life and led the ascetic life out of political discontent or disappointment.

(3) Legal Abdication.

I mean by *legal abdication* the compulsory loss of house-headship by way of punishment for a crime or other grave fault. Cases occurred very frequently during the Feudal times, especially under the Tokugawa Shōgunate, in which a house-head was sentenced or ordered to abdicate as a punishment for his offence. Particular names have been given to this kind of abdication, such as *zaikwa-inkyo* or "penal abdication"; or *chikkyo-inkyo* or "confinement abdication"; or *tsutsushimi-inkyo* or "reprimand-abdication." House-heads were also very often forced to abdicate by the resolution of family councils on account of their moral depravity, which made them unfit for the duties of house-headship. Even in the beginning of the present reign, this kind of abdication continued; and Art. 14 of the Criminal Code of 1873 provided that *kwazoku* and *shizoku*, or nobles and *samurais* who were guilty of crimes, involving grave moral depravity, should be sentenced to the loss of house-headship, together with their privileges.

(4) Physiological Abdication.

The decay of physical or mental power either on account of old age or ill health is the most common cause of abdication. Manu says—"When a householder see his skin wrinkled, and his hair white, and the sons of his sons, then he may resort to the forest" (Manu. VI. 2). As house-headship was an institution of *public law as well as of private law*, it involved not only power over the house-members, but also many duties toward the state, besides duties and responsibilities toward the house-members, which were incumbent upon that position. So, house-heads were often obliged to retire from the active duties of family life, when their age or state of health made them unfit for that position. This was especially the case with the *samurai* class during the *Feudal period*, *when physical power was especially necessary for the discharge of military duties.* It is for this reason that abdication came to be regarded as an important and necessary institution, and *laws relating to it made great progress under the military régime of Feudalism.*

The rule with regard to the *age* at which a house-head was allowed to abdicate was *seventy* before the establishment of the Feudal System, which was the age of retirement according to the Chinese Ritual Code. But *this age was lowered under Feudalism,* and *fifty* was fixed as the lowest limit of the age, at which a house-head was allowed to abdicate without adducing any other reason. But since the abolition of Feudalism and the establishment of the conscription system, which imposes military duty irrespective of a man's position in the house, there is no need to keep this low limit of age. *The new Code raised it again and fixed it at sixty;* so that there have been *three changes* as to the age of retirement, the first being seventy, the second fifty, and the third sixty.

According to the new Code, a house-head may abdicate when he has attained the age of sixty, but in case of a female house-head, she may abdicate irrespective of her age (Civil Code, Art. 752 & 755). In all other cases, the permission of a court of law is necessary. Such permission is given, if a house-head is unable to continue the management of the house owing to one of the following causes; namely, sickness, the necessity of succeeding as heir to the headship of the main branch of the family, or of resuscitating it, the desire to enter another house by marriage, or other unavoidable causes (Civil Code, Art. 753 & 754). In both these cases, there must always be an heir to succeed him in the headship of the house; for nobody but a person who has founded a new house may abolish it, as the abolition of a house would bring with it, in other cases, the extinction of the worship of the ancestors. (Civil Code, Art. 762 & 764).

ii. Loss of Nationality.

The house system is a *national institution*, and foreigners not being considered as belonging to any house, the house-headship necessarily comes to an end, when a house-head loses his nationality, by naturalization or other causes mentioned in the Law of Nationality (Law No. 66, 1899); just as a Roman *paterfamilias* lost his *patria potestas* on account of the loss of citizenship by undergoing *media capitis diminutio*.

iii. The Marriage of a Female House-head.

According to Art. 736 of the Civil Code, if a female house-head marries, the husband enters the house of his wife, instead of the wife's entering the husband's house according to the usual rule, and at once becomes the house-head, unless the parties concerned expressed a contrary intention at the time of marriage. Thus succession *inter vivos* to the house-headship occurs in case of the marriage of a female house-head.

iv. The Divorce of a Husband who has married a Female House-head.

As the husband entered the house and has become the house-head in consequence of the marriage, he leaves the house by divorce, and at the same time loses the house-headship. Thus divorce in this case becomes a cause of succession *inter vivos.*

v. Invalidation of Marriage or Adoption.

If a man who married a female house-head, or an adopted son or daughter has become a house-head, and the marriage or the adoption is invalidated for one of the causes mentioned in the Code, the husband or the adopted child leaves the house and the house-headship is lost. In this case, as the invalidation has no retrospective effect, the preceding house-head, though alive, such as the wife or the abdicated adoptive father, does not recover the house-headship as if there had been no marriage or adoption, but the rules of succession apply just as in the case of death.

The above enumeration of the causes will show that succession *inter vivos*, which is not usually found in modern laws, occurs very frequently under the present Japanese law.

XX

Conclusion

I hope I have been able to show, to some extent at least, that the new Japanese Civil Code furnishes valuable materials for students of historical and comparative jurisprudence. The Codification was the result of the great political and social revolutions which took place within a comparatively short period. The Code embodies in itself archaic and modern elements on the one hand, and Eastern and Western elements on the other. Within the past thirty years, Japanese law has passed from the Chinese Family of law to the European Family; the notion of right was introduced; woman's position was raised from a condition of total subjection to one of equality with man, as far as private rights are concerned; the status of foreigners advanced from the stage of enmity to that of equality with citizens; the family system was greatly modified; the separate property of house-members began to be recognized; and property succession has come to exist side by side with the succession of house-headship.

Comparing the new Japanese Civil Code with Western Codes, we observe great similarity between them in the first three Books relating to General Provisions, Real Rights and Obligations respectively, but great difference in the last two, which relate to Family and Succession. Of the first three Books, the law of obligations may be said to be entirely Occidental. That part of law may indeed be said to be in a sense cosmopolitan, the laws of different countries exhibiting a relatively small amount of variation in this regard. The law of obligations, therefore, has the greatest propagating capacity and is generally first received in other countries. Next comes the law relating to movables. But land is usually so bound up with the public policy and local conditions of a country, that we usually find much divergence in the laws relating to immovables in different countries. The laws relating to Succession and Family, depending, as they do, upon the national character, religion, history, traditions and customs, show the least capacity for assimilation. So, the usual order of assimilation, or reception of foreign laws is, (1) Law of Obligation, (2) Law of Movables, (3) Law of Immovables, (4) Law of Succession and Family.

I have not touched upon those parts of the Civil Code, which relate to Obligations and Rights *in rem*, because the rules relating to these parts are mostly derived from Western jurisprudence and will present little that is novel to a European or American audience. I have confined my remarks, therefore to those parts in which the indigenous element is usually most persistent. I have shown that even in these, we have made great reforms since the opening of the country to foreign intercourse.

During the last thirty years, we have been trying to adopt from Western civilization whatever seemed to us best fitted for the progress of the country.

We now possess a Civil Code based upon the most advanced principles of Western jurisprudence. But the Code is only a framework or skeleton of law. What supplies flesh, blood and sinews to it is the integrity and learning of the Bench and the Bar, and the law-abiding habit of the people. But, above all, the fountain-head of legal improvement is legal science. Law is national or territorial, but the science of law is universal, and is not confined within the bounds of any state. We have profited in the past by the work of scientific jurists of the West, and we must look, in future, to the mutual assistance and co-operation of the scientific brotherhood of the world.

INDEX

INDEX

INDEX

INDEX

INDEX

INDEX

INDEX

INDEX

大正元年九月一日印刷
大正元年九月四日發行

著作權所有

著作兼發行者　穗積陳重
東京市牛込區拂方町九番地

發行所　丸善株式會社
東京日本橋區通三丁目十四番地

印刷者　野村宗十郎
東京市京橋區築地三丁目十一番地

印刷所　株式會社東京築地活版製造所
東京市京橋區築地二丁目十七番地

定價金壹圓貳拾錢

学術選書プラス
5
民　法

✾ ❈ ✾

Lectures on the New Japanese Civil Code:
新日本民法典講義（第２改訂版）

2011（平成23）年６月30日　第１版第１刷発行
1255-6：P288　¥32000E-013：030-010-005

著　者　穂　積　陳　重
発行者　今井　貴　稲葉文子
発行所　株式会社　信　山　社
編集第２部
〒113-0033　東京都文京区本郷6-2-9-102
Tel 03-3818-1019　Fax 03-3818-0344
info@shinzansha.co.jp
東北支店　仙台市青葉区子平町11番１号208·112
笠間才木支店　〒309-1611　茨城県笠間市笠間515-3
Tel 0296-71-9081　Fax 0296-71-9082
笠間来栖支店　〒309-1625　茨城県笠間市来栖2345-1
Tel 0296-71-0215　Fax 0296-72-5410
出版契約　2011-1255-6-01011　Printed in Japan

 印刷・製本／ワイズ書籍・渋谷文泉閣
ISBN978-4-7972-1255-6　C3332　分類324-000：a005
1255-01011：013-030-010-005：P32000E
NDC 分類324.000-a005

学術選書プラス
5
民　法

The New Japanese Civil Code:
新日本民法典
Lectures on the New Japanese Civil Code:
新日本民法典講義(第2改訂版)

2011(平成23)年6月30日　第1版第1刷発行
1255-6:P288　¥32000E-013:030-010-005

著　者　穂　積　陳　重
発行者　今井 貴 稲葉文子
発行所　株式会社 信 山 社
編集第2部
〒113-0033　東京都文京区本郷6-2-9-102
Tel 03-3818-1019　Fax 03-3818-0344
info@shinzansha.co.jp
東北支店　仙台市青葉区子平町11番1号208·112
笠間才木支店　〒309-1611　茨城県笠間市笠間515-3
Tel 0296-71-9081　Fax 0296-71-9082
笠間来栖支店　〒309-1625　茨城県笠間市来栖2345-1
Tel 0296-71-0215　Fax 0296-72-5410
出版契約　2011-1255-6-01011　Printed in Japan

 印刷·製本／ワイズ書籍·渋谷文泉閣
ISBN978-4-7972-1255-6 C3332　分類324-000:a005
1255-01011:013-030-010-005:P32000E
NDC 分類324.000-a005

◇学術選書②◇

31 野澤正充　民法学と消費者法学の軌跡　6,800円
33 潮見佳男　債務不履行の救済法理　8,800円
34 椎橋隆幸　刑事訴訟法の理論的展開　12,000円
35 和田幹彦　家制度の廃止　12,000円
36 甲斐素直　人権論の間隙　10,000円
37 安藤仁介　国際人権法の構造Ⅰ〈仮題〉　続刊
38 安藤仁介　国際人権法の構造Ⅱ〈仮題〉　続刊
39 岡本詔治　通行権裁判の現代的課題　8,800円
40 王　冷然　適合性原則と私法秩序　7,500円
41 吉村徳重　民事判決効の理論(上)　8,800円
42 吉村徳重　民事判決効の理論(下)　9,800円
43 吉村徳重　比較民事手続法　8,800円
44 吉村徳重　民事紛争処理手続の研究　近刊
45 道幸哲也　労働組合の変貌と労使関係法　8,800円
46 伊奈川秀和　フランス社会保障法の権利構造　13,800円
47 横田光平　子ども法の基本構造　10,476円
48 鳥谷部茂　金融担保の法理　近刊
49 三宅雄彦　憲法学の倫理的転回　9,800円
50 小宮文人　雇用終了の法理　8,800円
51 山元　一　現代フランス憲法の理論　近刊
52 高野耕一　家事調停論(増補版)　続刊
53 阪本昌成　表現権理論　8, 800円
54 阪本昌成　立憲主義〈仮題〉　続刊
55 山川洋一郎　報道の自由　9,800円
56 兼平裕子　低炭素社会の法政策理論　6,800円
57 西土彰一郎　放送の自由の基層　9,800円
58 木村弘之亮　所得支援給付法　12,800円
59 畑　安次　18世紀フランスの憲法思想とその実践　9,800円

◇学術選書③◇

60 高橋信隆 環境行政法の構造と理論 12,000円
61 大和田敢太 労働者代表制度と団結権保障 9,800円
62 田村耕一 所有権留保の基礎理論 予8,800円
63 金 彦叔 知的財産保護と法の抵触 9,800円
64 原田 久 パブリック・コメント手続きの研究 予8,800円
65 森本正崇 武器輸出三原則 9,800円
66 富永千里 英国M&A法制における株主保護 8,800円
67 大日方信春 著作権の憲法理論 8,800円
68 黒澤 満 核軍縮と世界平和 8,800円
69 姜 雪連 信託法における忠実義務の歴史的・理論的発展
70 中西俊二 詐害行為取消権の法理 予9,800円
71 遠藤博也 行政法学の方法と対象［行政法研究Ⅰ］ 12,000円
72 遠藤博也 行政過程論・計画行政法［行政法研究Ⅱ］ 14,000円
73 遠藤博也 行政救済法［行政法研究Ⅲ］ 12,000円
74 遠藤博也 国家論―イェシュ、ホッブス、ロック［行政法研究Ⅳ］ 8,000円
75 小梁吉章 フランスの信託法 予8,800円
76 渡辺達徳 契約法の現代的思潮 予8,800円
77 山内惟介 国際私法・国際経済法(仮) 予8,800円
78 大澤恒夫 対話が創る弁護士活動 6,800円
79 村瀬信也 国際法論集 予8,800円
80 籾岡宏成 アメリカ懲罰賠償法 予8,800円
81 金久保茂 事業取得型買収と労働保護の法理 予8,800円
82 石崎 浩 公的年金制度の再構築 予8,800円
83 古川景一・川口美貴 労働協約と地域的拡張適用 予5,000円
2010 高瀬弘文 戦後日本の経済外交 8,800円
2011 高 一 北朝鮮外交と東北アジア:1970-1973 7,800円

広中俊雄 編著

日本民法典資料集成 1

第1部　民法典編纂の新方針

４６倍判変形　特上製箱入り 1,540頁

日本立法資料全集本巻201

① **民法典編纂の新方針**　発売中
② 修正原案とその審議:総則編関係　近刊
③ 修正原案とその審議:物権編関係　近刊
④ 修正原案とその審議:債権編関係上　続刊
⑤ 修正原案とその審議:債権編関係下　続刊
⑥ 修正原案とその審議:親族編関係上　続刊
⑦ 修正原案とその審議:親族編関係下　続刊
⑧ 修正原案とその審議:相続編関係　続刊
⑨ 整理議案とその審議
⑩ 民法修正案の理由書:前三編関係
⑪ 民法修正案の理由書:後二編関係
⑫ 民法修正の参考資料:入会権資料
⑬ 民法修正の参考資料:身分法資料
⑭ 民法修正の参考資料:諸他の資料
⑮ 帝国議会の法案審議
　—附表　民法修正案条文の変遷

信山社